A Woman's Insecurities

2nd Edition

Dr. Arletha Lands

Author's Tranquility Press
ATLANTA, GEORGIA

Copyright © 2024 by Dr. Arletha Lands

All rights reserved. No part of this publication may be reproduced, distributed, or transmitted in any form or by any means, including photocopying, recording, or other electronic or mechanical methods, without the prior written permission of the publisher, except in the case of brief quotations embodied in critical reviews and certain other noncommercial uses permitted by copyright law. For permission requests, write to the publisher, addressed "Attention: Permissions Coordinator," at the address below.

Dr. Arletha Lands
7118 Orral St A, Oakland, CA 94621, USA

Author's Tranquility Press
3900 N Commerce Dr. Suite 300 #1255
Atlanta, GA 30344
www.authorstranquilitypress.com

Ordering Information:
Quantity sales. Special discounts are available on quantity purchases by corporations, associations, and others. For details, contact the "Special Sales Department" at the address above.

A Woman's Insecurities / Dr. Arletha Lands
Paperback: 978-1-963636-90-1
eBook: 978-1-963636-00-0

This book is written in memory of my beautiful loving mother and other women who I have seen and experienced some of the most heartfelt disappointments and emotional let downs in their life. Also, to the woman who is strong but had no guidance on how to handle certain situations in many prominent ranges of emotional detachments that caused them to be insecure about themselves. In other words, handle it but keep the essences of hurt within their hearts, which made them become more insecure within their all-around self-image and self-worth.

I especially say to those women that are insecure, you are not made to defeat your own self- image or step on your own self-worth; but know that a positive mindset brings a positive self-image and self-worth. Many times, we as women are hard on ourselves and present negative vibes to cover our own insecurities. But if you know who you are and know your worth, try giving yourself more credit and defeat the oppositions. All women must recognize and know that the world is only great when you are in it and definitely can't survive without your presence of beauty, indigenous statute, elegance, breath-taking aspirations of motherhood survival, and most importantly, understanding that you are God's precious gift to the realms of society.

If no one ever tells you, HEY! Sisters, I love you all as well as want you to know how to handle the insecurities others try to implement in your life and really the ones we create and bring upon ourselves. So, stay strong, standup, except yourself, strive for proficiency, sufficiency, efficiency, and make living life in the most positive manner each day God gives you. "YOU GOT THIS GIRL."

—Dr. Arletha Lands, 2014

FACE-TO-FACE

WOMEN: WHY DO YOU THINK WE AS WOMEN ARE INSECURE?

"Because we have no consideration for our self-worth as well as understood that our self-worth is the core that establishes the foundation of confidence within our womanhood."

—Mrs. A.B.

"Because of our improper guidance on how we as women should handle things in life relating to our own confidence and because we do not have a positive mindset to want to do greater things for our self as well as how to treat the opposite sex."

—Mrs. E.M.

"It's almost scary to see and understand the issues that women suppress regarding their insecurities, and it's a terrific feeling to know we as women can overcome insecurity."

—Mrs. J.M.

"Well, I have just went through an insecure relationship and didn't really understand how low my esteem was until my health decreased because of it. So, I say because of our own mindset to think positively or negatively is why we are insecure."

—Mrs. Y.E.

Table of Contents

INTRODUCTION 1
INSECURITY QUIZ 4
THE DAILY MIRROR CHECK 5
MIRROR CHECK SCHEDULE 6
INSECURITY 9
WOMEN INSECURITIES 12
Emotional Security vs. Emotional Insecurity 14
The Positive Connection of Self-concept and a Secured Woman 16
Women Insecurities about their Physical Appearances: 26
Other Causation's for Physical Insecurities in Women: 32
Why Beautiful Women are Insecure: 43
Women Insecurities in their Relationship with a Man 46
Understanding what women want in a Man 49
Qualities Men look for in a woman 51
Most Common Issues Women Worry About in an Intimate Relationship: 52
Overcoming insecurity in her relationship: 63
Key Points for Overcoming Insecurity in Relationships 69
A Fear of Relationship Commitment: 72
Fear of Relationship Commitment Test 75
How can women learn to love themselves? 82
INSECURITY IN RELATIONSHIPS SITUATIONAL CASES: 85
WHO ARE YOU? 89
AFFIRMATIONS FOR BUILDING A STRONGER & SECURED WOMAN 90
7-DAY INSECURITY PROGRESSION TRACKING JOURNAL .. 97

INTRODUCTION

Before going on the journey of a woman's insecurity, I just have two questions: *Women why do we try so hard to change ourselves by belittling ourselves to please someone else? Is it enough that we devote our lives to others by making their life better than ourselves?* As women we just can't seem to pull it together unless we are step on by the same hopes and dreams, we wish for others, which becomes our biggest downfall. Our downfalls sometimes seek an insecure phenomenal journey which causes us to be in a state of being unsafe or insecure, which carries a load of self-doubt and deprived energies. Having that unsafe feeling and state of mind characterized by such self-doubt and vulnerability is definitely a mere fact in how we plague the quality of self. For instance, if we think low of ourselves why should you expect others to think any higher of you? You see, insecurity is said to be the antonym of security as well as holds a sort of uncertainty feeling that gives a lack of confidence or anxiety of self. However, when it comes to a woman's insecurities, the extremes of uncertainty and the lack of confidence go further than we think or even could imagine. For instance, women insecurities are denoted as a weak embolism that decrease their human worth as well as are tainted by all the selves she has in her self-image, self-dignity, self-respect, and self-perseverance.

See as a pattern in life sequences, women are raised with the understanding that their only job is to take care of the home, the husband, the children, do the "cooking" and keep up the good "looking", but in the process know what they want and need to make the struggles of life easier for the family. At this point, many women that carry this sequential pattern tend to forget about their own self-image and care for themselves. Moreover, insecurity not only destroys a woman's self-image, but it also deeply affects her mental mind-set, health, and relationships (with family, friends and significant other and the love of self). Yes, we are emotional creatures with unknown chapters that are not an easy task to read or understand. However, many times a woman's experiences either break or make her depend on the situational hand she is dealt. A woman's insecurities also affect the total content of the relationships she presumes. In relationships, insecurity is the root issue of most of the problems which can either tear it apart or just destroy the total core of it.

However, achieving the goals of an empowered security is not an easy task to develop without confidence. Because doubt will always be standing in the wings waiting to walk into your thoughts, making insecurity stand out, like it or not, you are the only one that can captivate its negative entrance. As women we should sometimes examine our behavior toward ourselves and ask ourselves what causes us to be insecure and how we as women can overcome the extreme measures of it? Furthermore, we as women must also understand that insecurities poses a habitual form of not being adequately guarded or sustained as well as know that it is even nervously insane of a woman's self- reception and standards of who she is as a woman, a queen, a treasure, a bouquet of flowers, a fresh ocean breeze, a milestone for many lives, a strength in drastic destruction, and most importantly, a sweet lily of the valley preciously created by God.

And just to know that we are preciously created by God; our focus should not be on our worth to the world but our worth to GOD. You see, you are worth more than your outer appearance, your job title, whether or not you can produce kids; how much money you make, your waist size, the color of your skin, what others portray you to be, fancy jewelry, brand name clothes and stuff you wear, and even more than what the world pressure you to be, a woman is a precious gift. Therefore, as women we should seek a secured phenomenon journey by securing our self-image, our relationships, know our self-worth as well as know what strength we bring to the beauty of life. Furthermore, as women we have a GOD given intuition to visualize with a radiant, clear, and free flowing spirit for building a stronger and secured self. To build a stronger and secure you, you should focus on these affirmations in your life: Self-love; Confidence, Powerful Feminine, and Empowering affirmations.

Before reading on take the "Insecurity Quiz" on the following *page. Maybe you will learn something new about yourself.* After that, then do the daily mirror check for 7 days, to see whether you hold a positive or negative self-worth and self-doubt. Later on, in this book, if you which to challenge your insecurity frame of mind, commit yourself to take the Oath of Security at the end of the book, by filling out your certificate of a secured accomplished woman.

INSECURITY QUIZ
(CHECK ALL THAT APPLY)

	1. I have to act just right and be perfect to feel okay.
	2. I don't feel good unless I'm making myself useful.
	3. I am envious of others sometimes.
	4. I always think I've done something wrong.
	5. I am sometimes a doormat.
	6. Looking in the mirror is painful for me.
	7. I exaggerate the truth or tell white lies to build myself up.
	8. I often worry about what people think about me.
	9. I feel like I'm always trying to prove myself.
	10. I sometimes feel like nothing, completely unimportant.
	11. I'm great at blaming myself. I'm my harshest critic.
	12. I can instantaneously tell you a list of everything that is wrong with me and why I'll never make it.
	13. If people aren't noticing me, I feel uncomfortable.
	14. I gossip and speak ill of others to feel better about myself.
	15. I feel incompetent and/or clumsy.
	16. I take compliments badly, either negating them verbally or in my mind or changing the subject and feeling uncomfortable.
	17. I have been abused either emotionally or physically.
	18. I take compliments badly, either negating them verbally or in my mind or changing the subject and feeling uncomfortable.
	19. I'm shy and not empowered to speak up for myself.
	20. I have money problems.
	What is your total score: _____

Scoring:
1-4   You are in a state of becoming unsafe or insecure and have some self-doubt.
4-8   you are losing your self-image, self-dignity and self-confidence
9-12   you have lost your self-confidence, self-respect and self-motivation
13-16   you are very insecure, have no self-dignity and can't trust yourself or others
17-20   you are not only insecure but have a low self-esteem, low motivation, not empowered, no self-perseverance and or negative of everything and everybody

THE DAILY MIRROR CHECK

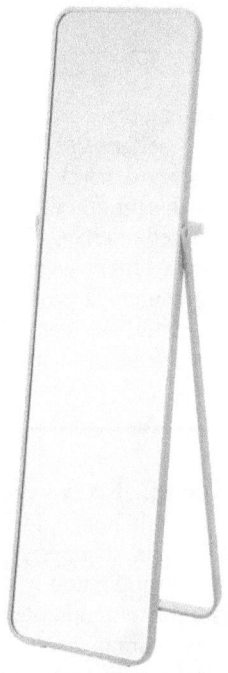

From this list of words, please circle what you see in the mirror about you on a daily basis?

Overweight woman, depressed woman, insecure woman, discouraged woman, low- self-esteem woman, low self-worth, low self- image, low self-dignity, a guilty woman, bad behavior, destructive woman, distractive woman, unfocused woman, non-determined woman, disappointed woman, jealous woman, beautiful woman, precious gift, anointed woman, blessing, assured woman, strong woman, a new woman, honest woman, secured woman, positive woman, good woman, empowering woman, a health conscious woman, go get it woman, powerful woman, high self-esteem woman, an encouraging woman, appreciative woman, improved woman, worthy woman.

Every day we are blessed to get up and challenge another day in our life. For the next 7 days, let's take a look at yourself in the mirror and tell what you see from the words listed above. This will let you know if you are living your life positively or negatively, be honest because that's the only way you can help yourself realize how to improve your self-worth and self-doubt. Buy a small personal journal or tablet and write down at least 5 words that describe you each day.

MIRROR CHECK SCHEDULE
(Please circle the word you see in the mirror about yourself on a daily basis?)

MONDAY:

Overweight woman, depressed woman, insecure woman, discouraged woman, low-self-esteem woman, low self- worth, low self-image, low self-dignity, a guilty woman, bad behavior, destructive woman, distractive woman, unfocused woman, non-determined woman, disappointed woman, jealous woman, beautiful woman, precious gift, anointed woman, blessing, assured woman, strong woman, a new woman, honest woman, secured woman, positive woman, good woman, empowering woman, a health conscious woman, go get it woman, powerful woman, high self- esteem woman, a encouraging woman, appreciative woman, improved woman, worthy woman.

#NEG: _____ #POS: _____

TUESDAY:

Overweight woman, depressed woman, insecure woman, discouraged woman, low-self-esteem woman, low self- worth, low self-image, low self-dignity, a guilty woman, bad behavior, destructive woman, distractive woman, unfocused woman, non-determined woman, disappointed woman, jealous woman, beautiful woman, precious gift, anointed woman, blessing, assured woman, strong woman, a new woman, honest woman, secured woman, positive woman, good woman, empowering woman, a health conscious woman, go get it woman, powerful woman, high self- esteem woman, a encouraging woman, appreciative woman, improved woman, worthy woman.

#NEG: _____ #POS: _____

WEDNESDAY:

Overweight woman, depressed woman, insecure woman, discouraged woman, low-self-esteem woman, low self- worth, low self-image, low self-dignity, a guilty woman, bad behavior, destructive woman, distractive woman, unfocused woman, non-determined woman, disappointed woman, jealous woman, beautiful woman, precious gift, anointed woman, blessing, assured woman, strong woman, a new woman, honest woman, secured woman, positive woman, good woman, empowering woman, a health conscious woman, go get it woman, powerful woman, high self- esteem woman, a encouraging woman, appreciative woman, improved woman, worthy

#NEG: _____ #POS: _____

THURSDAY:

A Woman's Insecurities

Overweight woman, depressed woman, insecure woman, discouraged woman, low-self-esteem woman, low self- worth, low self-image, low self-dignity, a guilty woman, bad behavior, destructive woman, distractive woman, unfocused woman, non-determined woman, disappointed woman, jealous woman, beautiful woman, precious gift, anointed woman, blessing, assured woman, strong woman, a new woman, honest woman, secured woman, positive woman, good woman, empowering woman, a health conscious woman, go get it woman, powerful woman, high self- esteem woman, a encouraging woman, appreciative woman, improved woman, worthy woman.

#NEG:_____ #POS:_____

FRIDAY:

Overweight woman, depressed woman, insecure woman, discouraged woman, low-self-esteem woman, low self- worth, low self-image, low self-dignity, a guilty woman, bad behavior, destructive woman, distractive woman, unfocused woman, non-determined woman, disappointed woman, jealous woman, beautiful woman, precious gift, anointed woman, blessing, assured woman, strong woman, a new woman, honest woman, secured woman, positive woman, good woman, empowering woman, a health conscious woman, go get it woman, powerful woman, high self- esteem woman, a encouraging woman, appreciative woman, improved woman, worthy woman.

#NEG:_____ #POS:_____

SATURDAY:

Overweight woman, depressed woman, insecure woman, discouraged woman, low-self-esteem woman, low self- worth, low self-image, low self-dignity, a guilty woman, bad behavior, destructive woman, distractive woman, unfocused woman, non-determined woman, disappointed woman, jealous woman, beautiful woman, precious gift, anointed woman, blessing, assured woman, strong woman, a new woman, honest woman, secured woman, positive woman, good woman, empowering woman, a health conscious woman, go get it woman, powerful woman, high self- esteem woman, a encouraging woman, appreciative woman, improved woman, worthy

#NEG:_____ #POS:_____

SUNDAY:

Overweight woman, depressed woman, insecure woman, discouraged woman, low-self-esteem woman, low self- worth, low self-image, low self-dignity, a guilty woman, bad behavior, destructive woman, distractive woman, unfocused woman, non-determined woman, disappointed woman, jealous woman, beautiful woman, precious gift, anointed woman, blessing, assured woman, strong woman, a new woman, honest woman, secured woman, positive woman, good woman, empowering woman, a health conscious woman, go get it woman, powerful woman, high self- esteem woman, a encouraging woman, appreciative woman, improved woman, worthy woman.

#NEG: _____   #POS: _____

COMMENTS:

DATE STARTED:

DATE FINISHED:

INSECURITY

One of life major challenges for women is becoming secured in our own skin and finding a positive self-image and self-worth. Humanly, it is understood that everyone experiences a form of insecurity, especially women. Although there have been many women leaders who have obtained a certain level of confidence and became role-models for many other women, the impossibilities of being 100% free of doubt are almost impossible because we are imperfect beings. However, the gaining of self-confidence is a gradual process and often comes with age and wisdom. Even though we are not perfect, being insecure is destructive and is the root of almost all problems. Insecurity brings about feelings of uneasiness which triggers a person to develop a lack of confidence, become inadequate and even to a point of trusting one's self or others. Insecurity affects your relationships making it hard to maintain your self-dignity and causes you to become withdrawn from others. Living in a world all by yourself woman is just a fallacy, wake up! There will always be other people around you. You see, being insecure affects your performance in all areas of your life and, mostly interesting, creates a negative mind frame against those who love you and care about you.

Being insecure, if you did not know, can even destroy your sexual desires. Just ask yourself, is it really worth it? Insecurity also affects your psychological makeup where you easily are agitated and hard to deal with, thinking you will become embarrassed or fail in any impeding decision-making skills, thus affecting your quality of choices. Many times, people are insecure due to their environment in which they are raised that is not conductive for learning and chaotic. Other reasons may include major setbacks or tragedies in life, a lack of direction in life; a lack of compliments from others and not being acknowledge; poor self-image; unrealistic expectations;

low self-esteem, lack skills and abilities; being overshadowed by successful people; lack of trust and jealousy in a relationship; and just a pure fear of rejection, pain, loss, and/or embarrassment. Some of the most common signs that indicate insecurity include bullying, excessive joking, self-promoting, and being too authoritative and competitive. For example, indications of insecurity bring about excessive joking done by people that crave to sort attention without understanding the limits of appropriateness; and bullying done by insecure people that tend to be threatened by secured people.

More specifically, people that are insecure find validation within themselves, whereas people who are secure find validation from other resources outside of themselves. For example, women who seek to find validation within them tend to become overly selfish and overly accommodating by surrounding their self with the center of attention, possessions and accolades as well as chose to gain approval of others and bend over backwards for them as a primary compensation definitely stems from their sort of insecurity. You see, people that are insecure can think of the many negatives of life's existence and that's because they disenable themselves from reality, while building a defeat of depression and lack of self-confidence. We still say to ourselves, but why are women so insecure? Well, there are many factors that can cause people, especially women to feel inadequate and have a lack of trust within self and others: factors such as

- Fear of rejection, loss and embarrassment which make them feel insecure and make irrational decisions in preventing things from happening.
- Not having realistic expectations were striving to meet the imposing of unrealistic expectations that are imposed by others.
- Been through a major tragedy situation in life such as divorce, the death of a loved one, bankruptcy etc.

- The environment in which they were raised hasn't had no conducive learning and chaotic.
- Having a poor self-image of their appearances, causing a degrading of self?
- Having low self-esteem, lack of skills and abilities.
- Showing jealousy in a relationship by not trusting others
- Become offended by successful people, feeling non-achievable than the next successful person.
- Having a lack of direction in the course of their life.
- Lack of being acknowledged and feeling unappreciated.

Now although these things are definitely true factors that impose within our lives, doesn't mean we cannot accept them and move on. Women we are stronger than what we give our self-credit for. Understand that insecurity is like an un-healing wound that you refuse to treat. Hey! Just treat it girl, so you can move on.

WOMEN INSECURITIES

Early we mentioned the many aliments insecurity brings. But Insecurity in women is expressed in different ways than men. For example, as women we are more emotionally construct which makes our insecurities difficult to spot, whereas men wear their emotions in an egotistical manner, feeling as defeated beats of revenge. In many women, the feeling of insecurity pops out in every phase of their life, especially in their relationships. Women who are secured within are more likely to achieve success, be respected and develop meaningful relationships whereas women that are insecure find the aspects of their life to be difficult and confining.

The feelings of insecurity in women often starts in their family origin issues and unhealthy past relationships. In many women, this type of experience could interfere and/or limit their ability to make better choices in finding success in life, a good partner, and positive friends. For instance, insecurity in a woman's family is more than a characterized mistake in how she responses to the calls of life, but it is the deep development of her rooted foundation where she was taught and created in the images of those before her. Believe it or not, the role of family provides a major impression in a woman's insecurities, especially in her self-image, self-worth, and in the development of her self-esteem. For instance, let's first take a look at the mothers in her family. Mothers are said to be the essence of how little girls are taught and raised. Mothers are looked upon as to be a strong confident and secured woman and caregiver. When you really think about it, being raised by a good and strong mother, we see them as the 'god' of making everything alright with any situation, even if we don't know how she accomplished the task. For example, mothers are looked upon as the all-knowing, the powerful one, the magician, the problem solver, the kiss the "Bo Bo" well, the caretaker, and however she mastered it we were infiltrated with those standards. In knowing that, we never thought to see whether her state of mind was secure and confident in the whims of her trials. As little girl's we tend to model what we see. For instance, if your mother had self-doubt and a lack of confidence in accomplishing any task, then I am sure you are 99% likely to have the same characteristics as she, not to say you can't change it. Moreover, even if a woman is raised by falser parents or extended family, the illustrations of their characteristics become set standards for their secured self-image, and self-dignity. Just remember, the bad that you think destroyed you can be a good thing to advance you.

On the other hand, fathers play a crucial role regarding insecurities or security in a woman's life. As women the majority of our perception for being secured in self as well as having that influence of strong confidence comes from what "daddy's little girl" need to positively sustain within womanhood. Although, a woman is said to follow in her mother's patterns of esteem, her self-security is also defined by the way her father treats her. For instance, if her father treats her like a princess, then a princess she is, and if he treats her like she's nothing than the traits of nothing she will be. For the most part, fathers have a strong effect on how a woman should be appreciated and her self-worth. In another instance, if her father treats her well and encourages her to reach for higher goals and aspirations, tells her to always know that she is beautiful, teach her to take no wooden nickels, and always keep her head up high, this is the stage setting of her foundation within her relationship to all men, especially with her boyfriend and/or husband. You see, although women are emotional creatures, we still hold up the world with our nurturing spirit and love for others, definitely being seen as an organized leader to life itself.

Emotional Security vs. Emotional Insecurity

Emotional Securities:

It is known by many that *emotional securities* measure the stabilization of a woman's emotional state of mind as well as provides a general perception in how she views herself and the vulnerability of her self-image. Women who are secured within themselves have the power to deal with negative life situations in a healthy and acceptable way. Although sometimes emotional security can be tested through the loss of a loved one, ended relationship, a divorce, and job loss, but if a woman is emotionally secured, has a high self-esteem level and confidence for herself can handle these experiences without some type of depression or other emotional issues. Typically, because a woman is emotionally designed, she will experience a certain level of sadness, worries and concerns but not stay in that place of her life. She will always find a positive stand to overcome the tribulations of being insecure. Siblings also play an important role in a woman's security. For instance, when elder women siblings show a strong source of emotional security in how they handle life-stresses, the process is copied and used within the functional lives of women after them. On the other hand, elder women siblings that shows a sense of insecurity inadequacy sets the stage for women after them. This type of emotional insecurity is implemented and learned which brings about a feeling of uneasiness in women that triggers a lack of self-confidence and trust for self and others. However, the concept of developing sibling insecurity can have a reverse effect on a woman's emotional security within her emotional state of mind.

On the other hand, *Emotional insecurities* are also related to psychological resilience which characterizes a woman's ability in adapting to stress and adversities. In other words, women having the ability to bounce back from arising difficulties of negative situations are less affected by such psychological resilience. Many times, women are triggered by bouts of depression stemming from negative situations which impacts a woman's self-worth, especially her respect and dignity level for herself. According to some psychologists, emotional insecurities does not only stem from previous difficult experiences it usually begins within a person's early childhood where the need for attention is yarned for and are not met, and emotional attitudes of unworthiness is developed leading to doubts regarding a person's abilities and anxiety about their interpersonal relationships.

Like I mentioned earlier, women learn from the women leaders within the family as well as use these teachings as a structured guide in their womanhood. These teachings provide a negative or positive influence to help women to regroup or regress in their state of mind; to feel unsafe or safe and insecure or secure about certain qualities that are adequate or inadequately in their life. "Food for thought," as women we should learn to appreciate and love our self and the foundation, we are built from whether good or bad; make the appropriate changes if need be as well as continue to improve and develop positive standards to better our own self-image.

The Positive Connection of Self-concept and a Secured Woman

A women's connection with creating a positive self-concept has many levels that she must meet to improve her security. You see self carries many features that are a prominent content to bring a positive influence on oneself pride, dignity, morale, self-confidence and self-assurance. These features reflect a woman's overall abilities to focus on five self-concepts that involve being a secured woman: self-esteem, self-image, self-efficacy, self-consciousness, and self-worth.

High self-esteem vs. Low self-esteem

Self-esteem is a built merging of character and confidence. Self-esteem can be categorized in two aspects: high self-esteem or low self-esteem. A high self-esteem equates to a positive self-esteem which allows women to reflect on their overall subjective emotional genre of what they are worth.

Women with high self-esteems seeks challenge and stimulation, willing to admit mistakes, act appropriate and openly honest, have high ambitious, and is willing to form nourishing relationships. On the other hand, women who do not carry such esteem are considered to have a low self-esteem of them and hide from the many challenges they are faced with. For instance, women with low self- esteems not only urge the need to prove themselves, but seek the safety of familiarity and undemanding, aspires to achieve less, over controlling, avoids risks, lacks clarity and honesty in communicating; bring destruction to their relationships, along with hostility, blame and a defensive mind

A *Woman's* Insecurities

set. Also, just a reminder to all women, self-esteem isn't how other people see us; it's how we see ourselves is what makes it hard. So, the self-concept we must endure at a highly devoted level is to develop a positive self-awareness that expresses our attitude of approval as well as extend our beliefs within ourselves that we are capable, significant, successful, and worthy. Other measures of self-concept in improving a woman's self-esteem relies within her honesty about herself, whether she likes or at least accept herself as well as willing to remove the internal barriers that keeps her from doing her best. As women, it is our own attitude about our self that encompasses our own beliefs about our self along with our emotional state of mind that includes the disparities, shames, triumphs, and pride that may create either a negative or positive evaluation of our self.

Because women are such unique creatures that deliver forms of self-expression such as attitudes, abilities, and emotions, we can either build our self-esteem or destroy it. In building our esteem, women must focus on positive aspects in life by setting realistic achieving goals as well as seek the company of individuals who are good role models, who limits criticism to a minimum. Now many times we as women destroy our self-esteem for some reason like wanting to compare ourselves to other women and then putting ourselves down. For example, when a woman looks at other women, especially on T.V. or at the gym, she sometimes becomes hard on herself because she doesn't look that way. But that's ridiculous! Because you are made specifically how God wanted you to be made as well as given what he gave you. Just be thankful that you are healthy and alive to live amongst the living as well as know you have a purpose that you need to focus on fulfilling. Another thing to remember is that you are a star in your own image, so girls use it to the fullest! Work more on building a high self-esteem by implementing these characteristics in your life; self-confident through enjoying good interpersonal relationships, being self-directed, being more loving and lovable, be rational, real, flexible and creative, independent, being able to manage change, having peace within yourself and accepting yourself unconditionally, knowing that you are worthy of living and assuming responsibility for your own live, being assertive and outgoing and most importantly, seek continuous self- improvement.

Self-Image

Another self-conceptual thought woman should seek to improve is their self-image. Today, trying to build and maintain a positive self-image is challenging, but can be achieved. Self-image is one of the most difficult resolutions that deliver the mental picture of a woman's resistance to change. You see the mental picture not only depicts or foresees the judgments of others but has been digested by the woman from her own personal experiences. Self-image is the perception of oneself. For example, women tend to carry their feelings openly around others which in terms aide in defining her personality, achievements, and values within society. On the other hand, women who have a high self-esteem carry a positive self-image that can improve their over-all quality of life. Self-image typically for women is mostly characterized as factors such as biological, social, or psychological. See building a positive self-image does not only improve your overall quality of life, but it also benefits your relationships. For example, when a woman is satisfied with her own body image a certain confidence and self-clarification in her personality become more esteemed. As for relationships socially, women with a positive self-image are clear about whom they are bring a higher conception of satisfaction and commitment to the relationship causing a certain level of investment in forming intimate bonds with their partners. For instance, when both partners develop positive self-images, it becomes more expressive and openly honest, making it more likely to have a secured love and trust within each other. Psychologically speaking, women that are engrained with positive self-images are more confident and

A Woman's Insecurities

comfortable about their sexual activities opposed to women with negative self-images who are self-shamed of their sexual encounters that leave them uncomfortable and non-fulfilling.

Fostering a Positive Self-Image:

Self-image is a dynamic changing process that occurs over a lifetime. That is why we as women should foster a positive one by first understanding its role in our lives. Understanding self-image meets the standards of all our intelligence, beauty, kindness, ugliness, or just says the assets to our strengths and weakness. To develop self-image is to learn its major impressible influences from our early childhood. See during early childhood we were molded by the characteristics of our parents, teachers, friends, and other caregivers. With that in mind, these types of relationships enforce what we think and feel about ourselves. For example, when we look in the mirror, we see their implementations for our lives. However, this may be a real or distorted view of who we really are and based on that gives us the development of either a positive or negative self-image. You see our strengths and weaknesses are adopted is why we act like we act today. As we continue taking in information and evaluating areas like our physical appearance in how we look; performance of how we are doing and for the relationship, how important you are, is a mere factor that we still have work to do. But the truth is if we focus on a positive self-image by recognizing and owning up to our own assets and potential with realistic intentions, we can boost our physical, mental, social, emotional, and spiritual well-being. So, to create a positive self-image is to first understand that it is not a permanent fix, it's a constant battle for change over your life span. Creating a healthy self-image first starts with learning to love and accept you first and then being accepted and loved by others. There are many ways we as women can develop a positive self-image:

Ways to develop a positive self-image:

- Define measurable and reasonable personal goals and objectives.
- Write down your positive qualities.
- Understand your uniqueness.
- Focus on your strengths.
- Love yourself by telling yourself daily.
- Think back to how far you have come.
- Refrain from any thinking distortions
- Give yourself positive affirmation.
- Check your self-image inventory.
- Explore and identify your childhood upbringing.
- Stop comparing yourself to others.
- Ask your partner to describe your positive qualities.

Now let's adopt an attitude that is in the realms of reality. A woman's attitude reflects her image, and the question becomes, how to make my positive self-image stronger? Well follow these steps and it will help you achieve that positive image.

- Look in the mirror and smile a lot
- Leave the criticism about you out of your mouth
- Make a list thing that you love and like about you every day
- Make sure you get your sleep on
- Wear beautiful and flattering clothes
- Make yourself look good at all times, regardless to where you are going
- Do interesting things that satisfy you
- Be yourself honey
- Girl just let loose and enjoy life!!!! You only have one!

A Woman's Insecurities

Body Image:

Body image is also a part of the positive self-image process. You see ladies, body image is more than how we look to others, it is part of what we think, feel, or react towards our own perception of our physical attributes. You see in our development of body image is affected by cultural images as well as family, peers, and other influences. For instance, if women allow themselves to think positively about their body image helps them to lessen any stress or depressive actions as well as keep them from any interpersonal anxieties which will help them delete any distorted thoughts that can contribute to a negative body image.

An important question is asked: How can we enhance our body image? Well ladies, let me break the news! Your body image is not on a fixed income as life changes, your body changes which makes you think, in order to maintain a positive body image is a lifetime series of actions or steps to take in order to preserve it. For the most part, body image is just a mere factor in how we think, feel and respond. However, there is nothing wrong with wanting to have a great body, but don't lose contact with the health of it. There are some ways we can enhance our body image:

- Love your body, you only have one.
- Make your body feel as comfortable as possible because that's your ride you know.
- Put your body through positive experiences; don't let it get beat down.
- Overlook any distortions you think your body has because some women don't have it, you're unique.
- Dress your body to its fullest potential; nobody can do it like you.
- Be your body's best friend to the end.
- Lastly, bring out the strengths in your body, while knowing your limitations

Self-efficacy:

Another positive self-conceptual process is Self-efficacy. Self-efficacy is one of the most psychology models that optimistically carry self-belief to its competence and chances for successfully accomplishing any task and/or producing an approved outcome. Self-efficacy provides a certain level of motivation, affective states, and actions that are based on a woman's beliefs more than what she objectively thinks is true. Women beliefs are very much curtailed by her confidence in her choice behavior, efforts, persistency, thought patterns and her emotional reactions. As women, we need to have positive self-efficacy in certain areas of our live because it helps us to know our worth. As Henry Ford famously put it, 'whether you believe you can or you can't, you are right.' And like Gandhi said as his pivotal role model: in how self-belief plays in our live; "your beliefs become your thoughts, your thoughts become your words, your words become your actions, your actions become your habits, your habits become your values, and your values become your destiny.

Well with that being said, if a woman is determining to have success in her life, she must focus on realistic goals by setting and aiming for them without working against them. You see a lot of times women tend to lose their own beliefs, by looking to others not realizing they already have it. So, we as women must understand that our self-belief is not just a psychological regiment as it relates to science but is a vital part of our daily life in line with our aims for success. You see the originator of this theory; Albert Bandura gives us four sources of efficacy beliefs: mastery experiences, vicarious experiences, verbal persuasion, and emotional and physiological states. Women whom have had a mastery experience are more powerful in controlling their success as well as inherit a stronger self- belief in overcoming various obstacles through their efforts and perseverance. In the second source of self-efficacy, women in their observation of people around them, especially their role models, tend to pattern after those they know have reached a higher success. For example, that old saying goes "if she can do it, so can I." In a sense these women beliefs are raised that they also have the capabilities to succeed. The third source of self-efficacy, women that has a certain verbal persuasion from people in their lives such as teachers, parents, supervisors, or other positive influential persons, tend to take on the knowledge that they pose certain capabilities to master things and can stand strong when problems arise. Lastly, in the fourth source of self-efficacy, a woman's emotional and physiological state of mind will influence her judgment of her own self-efficacy. You see many times women allow depression; stress reactions and/or tension interfere with their confidence in the capabilities to succeed. Furthermore, having such a mind frame shows certain signs of vulnerability which delivers a poor performance. But if we as women develop a positive emotional reaction allows us to boost our confidence in whatever the challenge maybe.

Self-consciousness:

Self-consciousness is a self-concept to feeling or having an undue awareness and knowledge of your own conscious being. Women understand it is an acute sense of self-awareness. Being self-conscious provides a sense of awareness that women should always take heed to, in their appearance and actions, especially within a positive realm of other strong women, who thinks the world of themselves and their success. But I truly believe if women can control their emotional perceptions of other women and speak and say positive things to build esteem and not take it down will bring a widespread to their own emotional maturity. See as women, the thing about having a self- conscious emotional concept can affect us in the way we see ourselves and thoughts to how others perceive us. For example, emotional concepts include pride, jealousy, and self-embarrassment. On the other hand, being self-conscious and self-aware can sometimes be a healthy sign of emotional maturity. For instance, having self-consciousness and self-awareness can help you to be more fitting and functional within your community, show good character, and have a feeling of remorse. However, the downfalls of having an excessive amount of self-consciousness can be unhealthy and create worst symptoms such as depression, anxiety formulating social anxiety, depression, personality disorder and isolation.

Self-Worth:

Lastly as self-conceptual process, we as women need to know our self-worth. You see self-worth is an important aspect in a woman's life. Having the sense of her own value and self-worth directs the way she views her human worth. You see the problems women have with their own self-worth is that their focus is based on measuring their self against others, rather than giving attention to their own intrinsic values. For instance, our competitive world tells us to be the best and better than the rest, that's what makes us feel good, but if you really think about it, no one is better than the other, we just have special features given by God. For that purpose, we are all equal, "I'm no better than you and you no better than me." We all bleed red blood. Because if we keep comparing to improve our self- worth, that's a fight that always will be a losing battle. Keep thinking, there are other people, better, richer, more attractive, or successful than we are, stop setting yourself up for failure and accept who you are and love it. Women your self-worth has external factors that can be harmful to your mental health. For instance, we as women base our self-worth on our accomplishments, appearance, and approval from other and when we don't get it, we become more stressed, angry, conflict even to the point of having eating disorders, becoming an alcoholic and/or drug user just to feel better about our self.

Although our accomplishments are important to acknowledge, building your self-worth should be taking as a unique quality that make you 'you.' Just remember rating ourselves is not the answer, just being yourselves holds the true value of your worth. One of the first steps to building yourself worth is to STOP comparing yourself to others as well as evaluating your every move. When we do those ladies, we are giving in to our *"critical inner voice."* You know that voice can feed you destructive thoughts about yourself and others even to the point of undermining your own sense of self-worth and making you feel even worse about you. As I was during my research regarding self-worth, I ran across an old article that spoke to the many reasons why most people are afraid of love. In this article written by Dr. Lisa Firestone explained in her article *"7 Reasons Most People are Afraid of Love."* In one of her statements, she explained how we all have a "critical inner voice." I thought to myself that is so truth. Because on a constant basis we have something negative to say about ourselves or others. She went on to discuss how the same critical inner voice inside our heads tells us sometimes how we are worthless and sometimes undeserving of happiness. And I thought to myself again, we do have a way of letting the psychological aspects of our mind take us on a negative pity ride. But you must understand that this type of mindset many times comes from our painful childhood experiences and critical attitudes we were exposed to early on in our life as well as the example of feelings of what our parents had which over time engrained in us. Many times, as adults we fail to see those engrained feelings as an enemy and instead accept their destructive point of view as our own rule of thumb. However, you can challenge your critical inner voice, if you just stop comparing yourself to other women and think positive. For the most part, try pursuing activities that are meaningful and lines up with your personal beliefs, and this will help you to develop your own sense of self as a worthwhile woman.

Women Insecurities about their Physical Appearances:

From a physical standpoint, women's insecurities about their physical appearances in most cases are related to four of the most prevalent common signs: weight, age, sexuality, and breast size.

Weight:

Weight is not only an obvious aspect of a woman's insecurity it is the dominant perimeters of her physical existence that drive the esteem of her societal presence. For instance, women who are considered quote unquote obese as society impress upon them, try hard to be skinny, regardless of how gorgeous they are, they see themselves as unattractive and undesirable, or for that matter not fitting into the realms of society. For the most part, these obese women are looking for quick ways to lose weight and/or trying anything that seems doable. Now I am not saying that weight loss is not a good thing but as long as it is healthy, why destroy the essence of your real physical beauty. So, what, if GOD gave some women more meat on their bones, but at least you have a body that is physically healthy. Women who are small, for example, 107 pounds or less is sometimes put into categories such as bulimia, anorexia, or just need to put more meat on their bones. See these are standards that make women feel insecure in her self-image as well as tampers with her self-dignity. We women really need to ask ourselves; do we want to be accepted for who we are? Are do we want to perpetrate an image we're not?

In the situation regarding men as it relates to your weight, there are some men who fall for the celebrity models, but real men know what's real. Men don't want "bone on bone"; they are looking for structure and comfort that contours a woman's body. There are men that love big women and those that love small woman. Regardless to your weight, GOD made a man for you. Weight is just a figurative negative societal impression on what they think we should look like, but if we really take note, as long as we are healthy and love ourselves being obese or skinny for that matter does not make us who we are, it's just an outward coverage of our soul as well as blessing to be made whole. Ladies, please appreciate your blessings because not every woman is as fortunate.

Age:

Age is a careful explanation that is also not easily given out by most women. Many times, women see age to be a concerning factor to how they are viewed and/or treated in society, especially by men. On one hand, women that are age 55 plus are sometimes jealous of other younger women because they want to stay looking young. For instance, why you as an older woman want to or even think that you can look 25 when you have already had the GOD given chance to shine. Let the young enjoy the young and stay in your own bracket. Because you had your chance, you are going to age darling.

Older women enjoy your life and show our young women life is beautiful. Now this works in reverse as well. Women that is young as 30 want to be older and become envious of older woman maturity standards. Many times, young women need to understand life as a whole because as you mature the knowledge about life can help you through your path. Also, if you are around a more mature and positive woman take notes because that which you may learn will someday save you the heart ship of life downfalls. But either way, rather you are an older woman or younger woman you should appreciate and live at the age you are given on earth and hopefully you live a blessed life as well as grow into maturity.

Ladies, know that when we accept our own self-image and age, we have made it too. There is nothing wrong with letting your age be known as well as having no reason to feel insecure. Age is mostly just a number but be sure you take care of yourself regardless. As you find that man in your life, if age is a problem for him, then he's not for you. Of course, you don't want to be aged 25 and he's aged 60. What could you possibly have in common besides fulfilling his sexual needs as well as being the flower on his arm to showcase? Is it just the money you're after? If so, just make a consensual contract, so you can get it honestly. But for the most part, just try and stay in your age bracket and wait until you mature and look forward to your years on earth. In another instance, when it comes to men, we women have either experienced it, saw it, or heard it, that young women look for older men and older women look for younger men to satisfy their own selfish ego. For example, your 62-year-old girlfriend dates a 31-year-old man, this is ridiculous to some women and exciting to others, but the key factor of respect and self-dignity is flawed because as older women we should be teaching our young men how to respect the young ladies in their own age bracket and not take them out of their own element of learning. Some people say age is not a big factor when it comes to relationships, but honestly, the experiences you had as you mature to the age of 62 hampers the mental growth of the young if not properly executed. So be careful in how you choose to step out of your age range more than 10 years, because you may be creating a monster of deceit against women, making it harder for our younger women to experience life at their own level, especially with a young man that's already been tainted by your older maturities that skipped him over his own gestation of life.

Sexuality:

Sexuality on the other hand is one of the most common types of woman insecurities. In other words, when it comes to women, sexuality is a capacity of her sexual desirability and power of possession. In many cases, women always want to be highly

A *Woman's* Insecurities

desirable, especially by her mate as well as measure themselves to other women who they think are more beautiful. For example, women *NOTICE* how their men look at other desirable women, which make them feel insecure as well as pressure them to work on becoming more desirable and competitive, they want to be the only desirable woman in his eyes. For the most part, looking sexually desirable than the other woman gives women an encouraged edge to knowing she got it going on.

Being sexually desirable also creates a test of self-dignity and self-image in a woman's credibility of how she treats her physical body. Making false changes, many women can't seem to get the point of their desirable standards, especially by the opposite male interest. For instance, women make the most drastic changes to their physical bodies just to call for greater attention. But in actuality, many women are confused in what beautifies their sexuality naturally. For example, women change their butt's, breast, and/or weight just to be noticed. But if we think about it, these changes are not what make you, it just changes your natural desirable essences of your sexuality to a make false coverage of the real you. Moreover, making physical changes to become more desirable to a mate is silly on your part and shows you're not comfortable with yourself. See most of you women think, just because a man looks at a very well proportion woman who has everything in place that that's what he wants. Yes, a man is going to look at a beautiful woman, that's in his nature. For instance, if she has beautiful legs, a nice round bottom, and a nice set of bulbs (breast), he's going to look and so are you. But this does not mean that's exactly what he wants or desires. Being desirable physically to a man, if you didn't know comes with your personality and then your physical beauties. For example, you can be one of the most beautiful and desirable women and have one of the ugliest personalities that will make you look ugly to him.

"Food for thought," yes, a man wants his woman to be beautiful and sexually desirable, but he also wants it to be naturally and not cosmetically composed. Women by making changes to your physical appearances to become more sexually desirable are not the way to go ladies. So be who you are naturally sexy desirable and stop the decoration.

Again, I say, "She just always measure her own sexual desirability against that of other women. STOP IT NOW!"

Breast size:

Breast size is one of the most ultimate misunderstandings a woman has in her mind. The size of a woman's breast holds a great deal of insecurity regarding her physical appearance. Women for the most part, seek to have a certain type of breast size they feel is more desirable to men. In many cases, women with small breast pray for larger ones and women with larger breast pray for smaller ones. Now which is it ladies? We have to know this is a major insecure matter that we bring upon ourselves. If GOD didn't bless you with big breast and gave you little breast, what is your complaint, didn't he give you some anyway? Many times, we try and emulate celebrities and models by wanting to look like them as well as start thinking those physical changes are more desirable than the real deal. But what it still boils down to is what we think of our own self-image and the self-doubt we have negatively digested.

What we need to ask ourselves, does breast size really matter? Is it a factor of our self-doubt? Are do we want to be something that we are not and give others, especially men the wrong impression of our body type and find out later he looks elsewhere for the real GOD given materials you are born with.

Pay attention ladies, you will someday get older and the breast implants and/or argumentations you spent so much money on will change in its own way. For example, if you had a breast implant at age 25 and now you are 55, changes will take place. "Food for

A *Woman's* Insecurities

thought," be thankful for what you have as well as have confidence in what you got, because there's always a man who will desire what you naturally have and treasure you for how you are "Graciously" made.

Being physically secured enhances a woman's security level as well as drives a positive image in how she spends time around her physical appearance. These positive images are reflected in the way she grooms her hair on a daily basis, whether she's at home or at the grocery store. Also wearing the appropriate clothing is an important aspect of our sexual orientation and desirability. As women we should always respect ourselves as well as wear appropriate clothing at our own maturity level and not her daughters. For example, if your daughter has on a cute skirt and she's 18 doesn't mean you wear the same skirt, have some self-dignity about yourself and know that letting your daughter see you dress like her just takes away the respect she has for you and level she put you on as her mother. Ladies continue to tell yourself; you are desirable and have sex appeal in your own way, regardless of what others say.

Other Causation's for Physical Insecurities in Women:

There are also other causations of physical insecurities among women. Two of the most intimate physical insecurities in women may include: Being attractive enough (Hair color, height, and eye color), and hygiene.

Being Attractive:

Being attractive is a major concern when it comes to a woman's insecurity level. Many times, women who are in relationships tend to, for some reason think their partner is no longer attractive to them anymore. So, what happens is that these women began losing excessive amounts of weight, get plastic surgery and even attempt to look like someone else. Is it really necessary? Because after this is done, you find out that your partner still isn't attractive to you. What do you do then? Does it spark your mind that the reason may be because it's not all about your looks? Sure, looking attractive is appealing to the eyes of men, but most important is how you carry yourself and the implications of your positive energies. Don't forget men love women who have self-confidence and project positive influence onto them. Women, if a man is no longer attracted to you, don't let this decrease your confidence because it's not you, it can be stemming from his own low-esteem. For instance, he might be dealing with a situation at the job, where he is demoted, and his ego is hurt. So, he may come home week after week seemingly showing no interest in you. Don't take any drastic measures to change yourself, just focus on you. As women, I know we tend to want all eyes on us, especially by our partner, but worry about yourself and put your energy toward you by staying confident and strong and eventually he'll come around or lose a good thing.

A *Woman's* Insecurities

For many women, hair is a major concern in how they look as well as their methods for making sure it's more desirable to men. Having the right hair style, the right color and the right length enhance a woman's security, but when the hair is not the way she thinks it should be, insecurities arise. For instance, women who have short hair want it to be long light-colored hair or blacker color and women who have long hair wants short hair that is fashionable stunning but wanting it to be good hair as they call it. WHAT IS THAT? GOOD HAIR! As women we must understand that hair is just an added feature to our personal appearances. If a woman seeks the attention of how her hair is accepted by people especially how men view her hair, then definitely the invitation to becoming a more insecure woman is mentally impressed.

Height and eye color on the other hand also sparks a type of insecurity in women. For instance, many women prefer to be taller than shorter because of their emulations of long-legged fashion models as well as hoping they can meet the desires of most men. But for the most part, being taller is not what makes a woman become more desirable, it's in how she present herself and the confidence she displays from her personal attributes. Eye color on the other hand, however, is also apparently an insecure issue that every woman wants to change, thinking that it makes them more desirable to men. For example, many women that have dark brown eyes try and emulate other women with blue, green and/or hazel eyes by wearing contacts, not understanding that their natural God given eyes works as well. GIRL those eyes were given to you, only to you, so be glad that you have them, because some women don't and most importantly, you can see.

Hygiene's

Hygiene's is one of the most crucial and critical but concerning factors that is humanly expected, especially in women. Women are one of the most hypo allergic creatures that define dirt and/or uncleanness as a sort of diseased experience. With that being said hygiene's play a major role in a woman's insecurity. Women with low-hygiene related insecurities stems from their emotional setbacks of self-doubt and low self-image. For example, a woman who lets her hygiene's negatively gets out of control lets down not only her personal self-image but pushes away any social involvement. Ask yourself, who wants to smell the funk of another human being, let's known a woman? The importance of a woman's hygiene holds great value within society. As the special creature made, especially by GOD to carry life on earth, to provide motherhood and security, we defeat our purpose and lose respect of the world and in the sight of GOD by becoming unclean and unpurified. Women it really doesn't matter what we are going through, please know that keeping up your hygiene's is the essences of your beauty and foundation to the next step in life towards a better relationship, friendship, and most importantly you, being that confident and strong vibrant flower.

Understanding the Mindset of an Insecure Woman:

Because insecurity is such a burden created by an emotionally destructive mindset, and is trying to deal with, it takes a vast understanding of a woman's self-worth and positive acceptance to conquer it. When it comes to a woman being insecure, she must first develop a positive mindset in order to deal with it. Confidence usually takes a gradual process and women who work towards gaining it creates an easier time in navigating positive life challenges. Although women are not perfect, it is easy for us to become overly insecure. We don't just become insecure we take it to extreme measures that are marked by an obsession for gaining approval of others. However, having such a lower level of self-doubt becomes an extreme destruction in our life as well as becomes the root of our problems.

A Woman's Insecurities

Moreover, when women develop an extreme search for security, they use the "overly rule" that manifests in various ways: women can become overly selfish trying to find their security through surrounding themselves with materialistic things and the demanding of attention; and become overly accommodating as their primary compensation in their attempt to gain approval from other people through bending over backwards. Without focusing on a woman's physical self, to understand the mindset of an insecure woman, there are some signs that indicate insecurity. The indications of these signs for an insecure woman include Overly authoritative, overly competitive, defensive, materialistic, disparage, and resentfulness.

Overly authoritative:

Being overly authoritative towards others and your partners can become cruel and negatively destroying. Women with such mindset tend to use their power in compensation of their lack of confidence. For example, frustrations are brewed, and unfair punishments are given out to prove her authoritativeness. In being an overly authoritative woman, you are a very controlling force as well as are very threatened by any satisfaction or validation without you. And as for your relationship, you think you are the only important person in life, and you will do anything to manipulate to get what you want BOSS! However, with such frustration, bossiness, and manipulative ways, you are building a fragile mountain to be shattered by an emotional breakdown that you will have. As far as your relationship with your partner is concerned, you are bound to be left by yourself without notice. Many times, we think being in an authoritative position puts us on top of everyone else, but in essence you dug the hole to the bottom of the barrow.

Overly competitive:

Overly competitiveness is another thing woman tend to think is okay when it comes to the opposite sex. Women with this type of mindset are very uncomfortable with themselves and have no respect for the opposite sex. You are a woman with no respect for men, the same ones you say you want, but put them down and crush their esteem to elevate your own. However, with such competitive attitude, if you have disrespect for self, disrespecting a man does not improve your self-image it just makes you become avoidable by others around you. What man wants to be around such crumbling mindset? And who wants to be around such sank attitude?

Defensive:

Women who are defensive are not able to handle criticism or any Argumentum conversations because she read too much into an innocent statement. You see women with defensive personalities always boast about themselves, talking to cover up their own self-doubts; feels a sort of resentment against someone, being jealous of how her partner may look at another attractive woman, which is her own fear of being traded. This resentment causes women to value herself less, have no confidence as well as have a low self-esteem; this woman even goes through her partner phone searching for other information. WOW!

A *Woman's* Insecurities

Materialistic:

Materialistic women tend to cover up their insecurities by buying things they can't afford and trying to keep with the JONES's. Listen! Not everyone is born with a silver spoon to have lots of money and things that really hold no value, because if you think about it, it can be here today and gone tomorrow. Now if you have a problem, don't spend money you don't have or can't afford, because when the bill comes, you will feel dumb and definitely broke to even pay your own bills. So, live at your own level of life, until God bless you to have more... but for the mean time girl, wear what you have because it's not what you have to wear, it's how you wear it, you see clothes don't make you, you make the clothes. Just think if no 'body' is in the clothes it just hangs there...LOL!

Disparage:

Now ladies, we have to be very careful in how we try and make other women feel because you know some of us got a bad habit of showing off in the front of other people, just to make ourselves look good. Stop acting like you didn't know that Janet didn't have nice clothes to wear when you guys go out somewhere. You see rather than helping each other as women, we bully and belittle each other trying to make each other feel small by dragging them down to our self-hating level, while destroying their self-esteem purposely which makes them a dependent, we built. No if you are a true friend, you would help build then destroy another woman's self-worth and self-esteem. Be the bigger person and show you have some type of self-dignity about yourself.

Resentfulness:

Now when we speak of resentfulness, that is very much a woman with low-esteem and very insecure within herself. Because any woman that expresses a feeling of bitterness or indignation of treating someone else unfairly is not a strong woman and definitely do see herself to be nothing but a low blood sucker of other women. If you find yourself in this type of mode, check yourself because nobody wants to be in your presence. Keep your entire negativity to yourself!

How insecurity affects a woman's health:

The effects on a woman's health can definitely be disturbed by her insecurity. You see even though insecurity is considered psychological, it attacks a woman's self-dignity and self-confidence which drastically affects her health. The health conditions we develop as women from being insecure in our relationships are far more serious than what we think. Research has even shown that secured healthy relationships help in avoiding illness, develop healthier habits, and have a life of longevity.

But to understand that it takes a woman with a secure and positive mindset and self-confidence to control how healthy she wants to be. On the other hand, unhealthy relationships do just the opposite. It stresses women the hell out, weaken their immunity and sometimes shortens their life span. Some of the most common health conditions caused by insecurity in a relationship: depression, anxiety attacks, stress, weight-loss, weight gain, high blood pressure, they go to drugs, become an alcoholic, not trustworthy, suicidal, unstable, lack of sleep, improper eating, and low hygiene.

A Woman's Insecurities

Depression:

Depression affects relationships in various complex ways. It has been proven to show an increase in the risk for clinical depression. For example, women who have been cheated on by their boyfriend, husband or significant other definitely become clinically depressed and at the breaking point of their life. But not only does depression create this breaking point, but it also triggers a full-blown case of generalized anxiety disorder. Anxiety as we know plays hand-in-hand with depression and definitely brings about a difficult situation when it comes to relationships. For instance, anxiety is generally diagnosed as a type of disorder that leads to an increased risk for social anxiety and is hard to untangle within relationship issues.

Generalized anxiety disorder:

A generalized anxiety disorder is described as a type of condition when people have experiences that stress them for no particular reason. In this case, generalized anxiety disorder is women who worry a lot, have no control, and become so irrational about a normal situation. Moreover, these women have a hard time functioning because of always being scared of not being financially stable, poor relationships, dealing with death, work, and family. But some of the health issues that come along with this type of disorder may include, she's always tired, a constant number of headaches, nauseous feelings as well as the development of pain all over her body. Is this really worth it?

Other health symptoms women with generalized anxiety disorder develop are rashes, hot flashes, have trouble with their breathing and swallowing. Many times, women who are in long-term relationships or have been married for a long period of time think that they develop depression and/or general anxiety in their present relationship, but the point is, you brought that baggage with you and just decided to let it out. On the other hand, as generalized anxiety disorder takes it told, a woman's social anxiety also kicks in. For example, women who experience social anxiety are mentally disturbed as they bring intense fear within their daily social situations. For instance, women who have been ridiculed and put down to her lowest develop a low-self-esteem that causes her to go into isolation, thinking it is only her that is going through it. Women know that we all go through traumatic situations that take us to the lowest on the total pole, but also know that that should pass just as everything else you have been through, and life gets better with experiences. Just a warning! Don't let depression and anxiety overwhelm you because it either leads to one or two things, drinking or drugs. All drinking or drugs will do to you is destroy your life. So, don't suffer your quality of life and know that there are other solutions, and hope, even if you feel worthless and hopeless, know that your life matters, that's why you are still here.

Weight loss and gain:

Insecurity also can affect a woman's physical condition by gaining weight. Weight gain provides a type of dissatisfaction in the relationship that stems from conflicts which leads to passive-aggressive eating behaviors and sleep issues in women. For instance, women tend to let themselves go after they become involved in what they think is a good and healthy relationship and start packing on the "happy pounds of love." But what some women don't think about is "the way you look when you got him, is what made him so attracted to you" In the beginning. Now don't get it wrong, you gain some weight and men still may love you anyway, but when he sees other women that look the same size you were, don't get upset if it gets his attention. Listen ladies, after you have put on those extra 30lbs, a man will still tell you that you look great, but when it's all done, you already know that he is not treating you the same or breaking his neck to look at you like he use too. So, get rid of those love pounds and do it healthy, not just for him but for you. As women, we should

A Woman's Insecurities

always want to look and feel our best regardless of what so men may try and do to our self-esteem; know that there is someone out there especially for you, weight, or no weight, we all have a preference.

Stress:

Insecurity can lead to higher stress levels which brings negative suffering to a relationship. For instance, women who are stressed drive a wedge between her and her partner. For example, having a negative attitude, dispute, disagreement over the finances, and looking at who is doing the most in the relationship, are known facts that increase stress. Having a negative attitude looks ugly on a woman. It destroys the viewing of your physical and mental beauty. A lot of times, the men we are involved in go out and cheat with another woman who is not always on his balls about simple things such as insecurity statements and questions. How long are you going to be? Make sure no bitch rides in my car? I hope she's worth it? If you are seeing someone, just tell me? See how stressed you made yourself? All that man wants is to be able to freely go and come back to you. Now if you know he is messing up with the finances, can't pay the bills, he's always gone with his boys, reducing the regular physical intimacy between you two, he stops giving you attention, and lying about things, then you have a legitimate reason to be stress. Now knowing this, you should try discussing these matters because this can help you relieve some stress. If these matters are not reconciled, it's time for you to move on, not stress.

High Blood Pressure:

Stress causes sleep issues that can exacerbate relationship problems and create vicious patterns, high blood pressure and most importantly kill you if you continuously let it be a part of your relationship. High blood pressure is considered one of the number one silent killer today. Having high blood pressure due to stress can be fatal, but why kill you? So, decide if it's really worth it, to be stressed or stressed free. The increase of drugs and alcohol usage is due to insecurity in a relationship, which does affect your health. Most women tend to consume lots of alcohol or do drugs when there is conflict and a lack of intimacy in their relationship. However, this can add more fuel to the fire of your relationship problems. Drinking and doing drugs does not solve anything. After you are full of alcohol and high on drugs, the problem is still there the next day. So, what's the use? To handle this properly, women you should get a grip on how you treat yourself as well as change your negative behaviors. Live life to its fullest!

Out of all the physiological and psychological effects caused by insecurities regarding a woman's health, mental health is the most extreme. You see mental health takes on a whole new form of complications. Mental health has various disorders such as anxiety, panic attacks, phobia, post- traumatic stress, obsessive-compulsive, major depression, impulse control, and substance abuse which all lead to drastic changes in a woman's life. At this point, you have gone too far, and you need help! So, try and understand if that relationship or situation you have been hoping for is not given to you, let it go, because it may cause more harm than you think.

Why Beautiful Women are Insecure:

Beautiful women have insecurities too. Many times, we think beautiful women have it made and that they are not worried about insecure things like how they look or the important quality of her attraction within society. Other women see beautiful women to be an idol of what they strive for and create this unrealistic mind frame that that beautiful women have it made because she's got everything going for her. But this is just an ultimate trap created in our twisted society. At one point, society set the phenomenal rule that, the prettier the women, the more advantages she has in making it to the top.

But we know that's just a figure of speech or an over-site to what a woman sees in her regardless of her beauty. Like the old saying goes "Beauty is Skin Deep." Sooooooo true. What we need to understand is that each woman is different and what she sees in the mirror about herself, beautiful or not beautiful is not everything society may see, but in reverse she tends to see everything she's not. We must ask ourselves, why is that? But she's beautiful, with a perfect body, smile, and hair just wrapped up in one beautiful package... Umm. Right! That's good she has all that, but does that mean she is psychologically accepting it, or even knows what to do with it, or just doesn't see it because of the many triumphs in her life experiences.

You see many times being beautiful can either make you or break you! But for the most part, women who are beautiful is very critical of themselves, some even develop sink and vain personalities; these types of women, believe it or not, build their esteems off crushing the next woman's esteem. WOW! We can say that all day, but the truth is, these women have a deep sense of insecurities, rather it's her eyes, nose, lips, hair, color of skin etc.... you name it, it's there.

So now that we know beautiful women have insecurities, why is that? Well, because these women are constantly complimented, I think an insecure complex is encouraged where she feels placed on the highest pedestal and is judged solely on her looks, which makes her feel that is the most scrutinized quality she has. This, however, formulates an emotional and physical standard for her to compare herself to other beautiful women. For instance, she's pretty and fine as wine, but not as the other women she sees to be prettier or finer. However, in reality pretty is not doubled, it's just plain old pretty. Looks are part of a woman's physical appearance and there is no control in how we look because God made us. You see the quality of a woman's beauty is attained and not conditioned by societal figures. This is the main reason why beautiful women are safeguard in their physical qualities that will soon decrease with age. There are two good reasons I think why beautiful women are insecure and become paranoid and hold competition to other women:

1. *The terrifying fading aspects of temporary physical appearances:* A beautiful women fights on a daily basis to not show a decrease in her beauty. Because she has the idea that looks are all she needs, she strives to look 22 years old even when she's 42 years of age. This is why insecurity set in. "she has it now, but loses it later," with the physical changes of life, which is the way GOD intended it.

2. *She's constantly being judged on her looks and believing that's all she has to go on.* Many times, beautiful women worry about how people see their outer appearances and what their expectations are of them. Because she knows beauty right now is all she has, but not looking at or recognizing that someday she would lose this beauty, whether in age or other uncontrollable situations such as,

A Woman's Insecurities

car accidents, physical abuse, and/or fire. All she knows is that her beauty is her survivor tool, for what she thinks.

Being a beautiful woman can sometimes seem to be a curse but understand that you are created in your own equal of your own human design. The primary adjectives for what a beautiful woman should focus own is self-love and positive self-dignity. See to love yourself does not always grantee you that everybody else is going to love too, but it provides an outward expression of your secured happiness and how you're in control of the love you share amongst others around you. By having strong and positive self-dignity shows how you as a beautiful woman are secured in who you are, how you look and your beautiful contribution to society as a whole. *SO, YOU SEE, BEING BEAUTIFUL IS A CHARM TO THE WORLD WHICH REFLECTS OUTWARD AMONG SOCIETY, BUT BEING BEAUTIFUL INSIDE IS INCRIDIBLY A BLESSING REGARDLESS OF WHAT THE WORLD THINK OR SAYS, NOTHING CAN TAKE IT A WAY!*

Women Insecurities in their Relationship with a Man

Women who are insecure within their relationship with a man can lead to a field of destruction. This type of destruction causes a constant struggle for control and energy. Many times, women who are controlling end up being attractive to other controlling people, especially men. You see insecurity can only bring fear-based emotions that prevent trust in a relationship. Insecurity in a relationship not only paralyzes its oneness, but shatters the GOD given answer to a woman and man existence on earth. For instance, insecurity creates a perfect storm that forfeits trust to be never established nor proven. In many cases, insecurity in women stems from having a lack of love in oneself and a feeling of rejection. Women who have this type of mind-set believe that if they find themselves unlovable, so must that man and began to create scenarios of rejection that is based on their negative beliefs.

Conversely, the highest point of a healthy and vibrant relationship is its trusting abilities in one's partner. We as women must understand the importance about sex, financial security and exhilarating thrills are not the only requirements in a relationship and does not replace trust. Because without trust all of your requirements are not attractive, and your relationship has no survival. Moreover, when trust is established, your intimacy level flourishes by becoming more intensified and emotional, if you provide a firm basis and support where trust can exist, it will allow your man to breath freely and relax in the relationship.

Another reason why women is Insecure in a relationship with a man beside trust could be that of their poor self-image or low self-confidence, past infidelity; or wanting to know is the grass greener on the other side mind-frame. I know I said a lot here, but just think

A Woman's Insecurities

about it. Many times, women use "play jealous" as a sign of affection for their partner, but that are actually just a sign of her insecurity. The jealous women mindset for the most part stem from fear or being alone or not being good enough for that man. We harbor so much negativity in our mind that we tend to lose ourselves which is why when women who are in their relationships tend to think they are not good looking or see their man look at another woman and feel they are lacking something in some way or another. You see this has a lot to do with a woman's self-image and self-confidence. Look all women are beautiful and created in a very special way. Women must be happy and see the beauty within them and know that no one is perfect. Another reason some women have insecurities in their relationship with a man is because of her past relationship, where she experienced infidelity. For instance, it may be a past infidelity within a relationship where the man was unfaithful. Just for this reason many women tend to feel a sort of insecurity in their relationship to a new male partner. Mental check girlfriend. However, you need to realize that this is a new man and not the man from your past experience. "Let it go girl."

Now many times women tend to wonder about having relationships with men who look like they got it going on, while overlooking what got him going. This is where women make that great mistake. Even though someone else's relationship may look good on the outside, does not mean it's good on the inside. Just look at some of you women wondering about somebody else's grass. Well, wondering if the grass is greener on the other side is definitely a major cause of insecurity in a relationship. As women we tend to get hung up on another man's characteristics and think we vibe the same, become involved and shocking to realize it's the same characteristics we got away from in the past relationship. This can be especially damaging as well as cause mixed vibes and vice versa in your present relationship. So, if you want that relationship try and reduce your insecurity and work on your self-esteem. Remember, if this is not done, jealousy will always cause insecurity and the problem will continue into every relationship you have. Keep this in mind, give your new man a new start, you never know what good it brings and if you are not willing to unclog your mind from the past relationship, leave people along until you clear yourself.

Understanding what Women want in a Man

Women who have an understanding of what they want in a man is not always truly thought out, because each relationship she encounters changes her perspective in what she is looking for. For example, she meets a man with good qualities but has no self-respect for women or even knows how to treat a woman. Then she meets another with a family caring background and wants children like she does but doesn't have a job or is looking for one. Then she meets Mr. Right, she thinks that has a good job, family values and gentlemen characteristics, but is depressed and angry for his past experiences in life with a woman or his mother issues. We can go on and on, but understanding what a woman want in a man has to be determined within her present relationship, not her past. You see women who have a good understanding of what they want in a man, will be able to understand that men are creatures that look at other women, not because they want them, but it's their nature; men flirt with other women when speaking just to test their ego to see if they still got it, not because he wants that female to be his; men play mental games because of their need for attention by having you think something is going on when they really have nothing going on; giving you the illusion that a female at work is interested in him by telling you what she said to him, or other women at the store and anywhere else gave them a compliment on their hair, clothes, shoes, physical structure, they take it to the bank. See you have to learn to look over our 'little boys' syndrome, because he just wants to make sure you still want him. But for the most part; understanding of what you want in men should be determined on how he treats you, are there any future plans, do you have some of the same goals in life, and do he want you for you or just for what you have going on. Let's turn it around, do you want him for who he is, what he has or his materialistic possessions. You want in a man shouldn't be materialistic or physical; it should be because he makes you happy and fulfills that gap in your heart that you can cherish. So, make sure your wants and needs in a man is a positive reach because reaching for something that looks like 'gold' can quickly trick your mind and set it on 'copper' which is not bad but less than what you bargain for. There are several qualities women want when finding a good man: she wants him for specific traits such as his character, is he faithful, dependable, or kind; what is his personality like, do he have a sense of humor, is he passionate, is he generous, or have intelligence and confidence; do he have the skills to listen, be romantic, have any cooking or cleaning skills or even any earning potentials; is he handsome, into fitness or have a sense of style. You see women want specific to romantic partners who treat them special and fair, equitably for the most part. Women value trait

Qualities Men look for in a Woman

Men seek certain qualities in woman that holds them together. What do I mean? Well, many times men want women that have a beautiful physical attraction and are employed to take off the pressure of not feeling used or becoming overwhelming with responsibilities. That's fine and all! But men really are looking for their mother to be honest with you. I know some of you women have even been told that you act like their mother or aunt 'Betty'. But the true fact is that when men fine women that possess some of the same qualities of their mother, they seem to cater more to that woman because of her motherly wit possess, which makes him feel wanted and loved the same. I wish we women can do something about this, but hey this is what we have in life, and I know we are stronger enough to handle our baby boys.

Some of the main **traits** men want in a woman includes: her independence, affectionateness, kindness, sense of humor, intelligence, her character, definitely her confidence, opinionated, and negotiable. But the top **qualities** men want in a woman goes a bit deeper than just these traits. Although some are interchangeable: he wants a woman that is kindhearted, family oriented, ambitious, intellectually challenging, consistent, understanding and empathetic, that has a willing spirit with effort, has similar values, loving and affectionate, friendly and sociable, physically attractive, and has a sense of humor.

Most Common Issues Women Worry About in an Intimate Relationship:

Besides the most common insecurities regarding women physical appearances, women also have insecurities in their stability in an intimate relationship with a man. Insecurity is an intimate relationship is one of the trickiest relationship issues that create a self-perpetuating cycle. For instance, women who are insecure in their relationships tend to make matters worse by pushing their partner away, especially in intimate relationships. You see when women enter intimate relationships with men, they become very emotionally vulnerable, especially if they have been let down or hurt from previous relationships. Therefore, the typical thoughts and feelings of having a habitual and problematic insecure partner involve a whole lot of issues.

Some of the common issue's women worry about why in a intimate relationship with a man include matters such as, being called back after a date; sex is all he wants; he's involved with other women; he lost his attraction for me; not having enough money; and not intellectual enough. Well let's talk about these matters, so I can tell you what to do Ms. Lady! And stop worrying!

Being called back after a date

See a man knows when a woman is strong and has her "A" game together. If he wants you and on your first date you didn't give up the *"jewel"*, then he will call you because it is a challenge to his ego to see how easy you are and the type of self-respect and control you have for and over yourself.

A *Woman's* Insecurities

However, if he just choice not to call you back, this is not the end of the world. He's definitely not the only man GOD made. In many cases we as women tend to put all our jewels in the same basket and lose a couple on the way with rushing something that we feel is love at first sight. However, if you feel that you and that man hit it off right and he don't call you back when you think he should, it does not mean he is not interested, he is probably getting out of another relationship or just being cautions.

Many times, men are checking out your attributes and not you contributes to him. See he just wants to know your personality, how you view things and your interest, lets him know if it's worthwhile for him to devote some time to it.

What to do? If that particular man did not call you back, so what? You just keep holding your head up and keep your priorities in check and know that it's his loss. Do not break down and call him first because if he's interested you will get a call. Girl a man looks at that and sees either a "needy woman" or "gold digging prospector." So, don't do that to yourself, honey just like you caught his attention, the fish didn't stop biting, they're just in a different location. So just go on with your day, keeping everything, he likes about you to yourself but stay friendly. And for the most part, why are you worried about him calling you back anyway, he's not the only man GOD made for you, and definitely the only one who have a phone. I believe it's a myth to say, "there are few good men available" and a "hundred women-to-one." As long as I am living and even having my own children, boys' and girl's children are born by the thousands, even in doubles; and some are even born at the time we are. I truly believe "what is for you will be" and "if it's not for you, keep it moving."

Sex is all he wants

Women in every aspect of a man, sex is the first attraction. "It's not their fault, they are made this way! The increased sexual desires of men have to do with his high level of hormonal testosterone. By nature, men is made to seek a lot of sex, while women is made to seek better admires in making better choices. It has been said "Men seek quantity and women seek quality." Men become very frustrated with women because they want sex and we talk about love but don't want to make it. Because sex to women is a culmination of her emotional commitment to a man, she looks for some assurance to make sure he sticks around. In most cases, when a woman is insecure and needs attention, she uses her sexuality to attract the man she thinks she wants. Giving up the "ruby" to a man is not new to him it's just a different "ruby" with the same feeling. Sex is a physical act that only eases his testosterone pressure and after that he may experience some type of love for a woman.

Get that woman, I said **"MAY."** Listen every woman have a set of "rubies" to offer, your ruby is no better than the other ladies, so having sex with a man is just part of meeting the aspirations of his sex drive, not his brain. In many cases, after a man has relieved his testosterone pressures, often they disappear because they got what they wanted; definitely we know it wasn't love. Ladies sex to men is just a mere check of their passion, not love. So, having sex early in the relationship is not only hazardous for your self-worth but it lowers your standards of even having a chance for him to develop any romantic feelings for you and/or a promising relationship. Having sex attainable, but not quite at the peak of its sexual tension can be mind-blowing as well as lay a proper foundation for a future relationship and love. Women you are better off understanding that men fall in love through sex, and we are the opposite. But it's not the physical sex that gets him interested in you, it's the *"social evaluation x-ray"* (sex) of your mind that drives him. Did you not know how sexy your mind can be?

A Woman's Insecurities

What to do: First women hold on to your 'jewel' and don't let it shine unless that man shows you, he is interest in delicately and preciously caring for the 'jewel.' You are doing this just to make sure that he is not just attracted to your physical sexual appearance and trying to get you laid quickly. See if a man tells you he loves you in the first few weeks of your dating cycle; ignore it because it's just his testosterone pressure rising from his small head to the big head. And even if he showers you with flowers and gifts, it's just the pressure of sex on his mind. But also understand, if you put it out there in the way you dress, the way you carry yourself and even in the way you hold your conversation, if he can get the sex first, he will. Women make secured choices in who you deliver your 'jewel' too and know that it is your "pride and joy" in the strength of your womanhood. Man can only get what you give them! SEX is overrated, but good with the right person.

He's involved with other women.

Women before you met that man of course you knew that he has been with other women from the past and is still in the present. Rather, it is the ex-girlfriend, ex-wife, the mistress, or the baby-mama drummer, a woman is present. Do you really think a man just mastered the knowledge in how to handle a relationship with women just when he met you? Let's think! Men are like creatures of the wild, they look for the weakest link of their women prey and immediately penetrate into the missing slots of a woman's emotional concerns. Now that almost sounds like love! And with that being said, there are many women who accept men anyway: married, involved, or just a trick to fulfill their sexual cravings and emotional needs. However, these type women are women with low self-esteems and self-worth, accepting any piece of a man they can get because they are lonely. Women you must understand that a man's ego thrives off his involvement with you, particularly sex. They are like a kid in a candy store, trying to eat all the candy and not find one piece to keep for later, he wants it all until he realizes one is good enough. Women we are his world and help mate to meeting the challenges of the world he faces on a daily basis. In many instances, women involve themselves with men that they consider the idea of being fine, built, and handsome hunk. So, we go for the "O-ke-doke". First, we can't believe he's attractive to only us. And just when we let him continuously stay over or move in after only dating for a few months, sexing him with our 'jewel', giving him all of you, receiving him in our heart, and thinking that this piece of hunk of a man is all yours, the cell phone starts to ring late nights, he starts to make excuses for not coming over, and he starts hanging out a lot with the fellows every Thursday, Friday, and Saturday nights.

Well, if this does not peak your suspicions, your insecurities have gotten the best of you. When a man is involved in one or more relationships, not that you are looking for signs, but the signs are there.

Listen, how we know a man is in another relationship? When a man gives you a lot of attention and treats you like a queen, you can call him anytime day or night, and he always checks on you to make sure you are fine, then all of a sudden, he stops giving you that 'queen' attention, he starts calling you less to check on you, he starts making up excuses to not come over and most importantly, he began lying about where he is, there is another 'booty on duty.' See in the beginning your booty on duty has worked the hours he needed you for and now he goes on to employ the "New Booty" and your shift is split and hours are reduced. Many times, insecure women see those signs but overlook them because she wants to keep that man. But understand sister that you are not keeping that man he's not yours and never was. Please open your eyes and see you are just threading yourself alone by keeping yourself for a womanizer and missing out on other opportunities that may bring the right man into your life, who wants you for you and not just as a convenience. Also, in this very same situation, women with low self-esteems accepts this

A *Woman's* Insecurities

womanizer type of man and tend to worry about who is the best woman when she knows there is another woman, but to worry is just a negative interpretation of your self-worth and self-dignity.

Men are somewhat always involved with other women, it doesn't matter where he resides *(job, store, doctor's office, gas station, hospital)* he thrives on meeting women just to see if he still has it. STOP worrying girl, he sometimes does stuff just to make you jealous. So, if you give him that power of control, he uses it to his advantage by keeping you worried and leached by his strings. Men who are involved with other women when taking you to meet his family, if at all, will take you to his sister house, his aunt house, his cousin's house, and only to his mother house if he considers you to be a decent woman. So, in other words, he will never take you to his own house and if he does it will be around lunch time or in the evening when he knows his wife, girlfriend, and/or other partner is at work or out of town. We say it's hard to tell that a man is involved with another woman, but it's really not, the signs are there, just pay attention to the conversation and presentation and not your feelings of emotions for him. You see men tend to make the biggest mistake when it comes to their involvement with other women by locking his phone, secretly buying a new phone, hiding his wallet, lying about their work schedule, using his friend to cover up for him about the next girl, coach the other woman when and where the woman is coming and where she is going to be, and just overall trying to be slick.

What to do: women if a man is involved with other women, it is your duty to disengage from any physical contact, but still, you can be friends. Please take this precaution because if you continue to have any physical involvement, your health could be at stake. Also, if a man tells you he has a wife, girlfriend or partner, just think about yourself being that person and respect the next even if you know them or not. Also think about if he is lying with you and his wife, then who else is he laying with besides you two. Now that's just nasty and dangerous! Even though some women know this they sometimes can play some dirty games that can hurt you. They may think they're hurting the other woman, but they're really hurting themselves, because that man still leaves them and go home and in most cases the wife is not worried because when she catches him and divorces him, she gets her part and even her heartaches and worry is over and she thanks to you, you have taking them away, by getting that man. So be careful in being the other woman "what looks green on the other side is not always green." If a man is involved with other women and you are really interested in him, let it go, you don't want the problems that the present woman has. Look don't let a man just tell you he's getting a divorce, he just broke up with his ex-girlfriend, he's married but they are separated, believe nothing without proof because "showing is believing." Just remember there is always someone for the other person, it just might not be time for you to be involved. Just wait and not try.

He lost his attraction for me.

Women if a man become less attracted to you, when you know he was at the beginning means someone else is holding his attention or something is negatively affecting his self-esteem. For example, it can be a co-worker, someone he sees as an opportunity to meet, or someone who listens and/or gave him what he wanted, like you did in the first place. For years we thought men are attractive to female statuses based of their youth, beauty, and virtue. On the other hand, it could also be another woman that challenges his ego with her youthfulness and excitement about life. Women also tend to be programmed in pursuant of a man status (how much money he has, what kind of car, does he have a house etc....). Needless to say, a woman thinks her appearances (weight, make-up etc...) may be the reason for a man not being attracted to her anymore. But in actuality a woman's attractiveness that sets within is what he really wants.

A Woman's Insecurities

You see women are always searching for ways to make them more attractive to man without feeling some type of resentfulness about it. But women with secure self-knowledge have a greater respect for themselves on many levels.

Many times, women become angry and indignant, worrying about losing her self-respect. But taking drastic measures to change self still does not guarantee that he will find you attractive. So often we women address our outside and forget about what we gave from the inside. If you are a secure woman that carry yourself respectfully and project positive energy, showing that you have that confidence and make a man feel good about themselves (not baby him) your attraction is "boldly" accomplished. Women who are insecure tend to think negatively about her by wiping out any confidence she may have had and when she meets a man, this means that she will potentially look to a man to bring up her self-esteem. However, women need to be very careful in how we look at attraction because attraction is not always about looks; it's about confidence, self-expression, and the way you make yourself feel. Let's not get it confused, how you take care of yourself women are definitely a plus because it brings a unique attraction in your perception of self-image. Women with your career-oriented self can also be the problem in a man having no attraction to you anymore. You may ask yourself, how is that? Well, many times women who are career-oriented put off marriage, having a family, put their relationship on the back burner and mostly think about how far they can get up the corporate ladder. But sooner or later, when they think about it their biological clock is expiring, the relationship is over and they become lonely and desperately looking for a good relationship, when they already had it. Another very important point as to why he's not attractive to you anymore may not have to deal with you at all. Work can be causing a man stress where he brings it to you. But this may be just a mere fact of him having a low self-esteem from his job and nothing to do with you.

What to do: So, focus on you and stay confident in the choices you make because no matter what, rather or not if he may not be attractive to you, someone else is. Instead of changing your appearances, focus on becoming attractive in your present and being an enthusiastic woman. See women, men are like babies who need attention and want women who prioritize the closeness and intimacy in the relationship as well as want to know they matter. So, without overdoing it, you can still show a certain devotion to show your care and investment. Don't contribute to that whole unattractive business and stop focusing on pleasing him but also focus on pleasing yourself. The true fact lies in do you think you are attractive, not what he or anyone else thinks of you. You are a queen, act like it.

Not having enough money.

Women every woman wants to be financially stable, but your financial status or career doesn't enter into the equation with your relationship. What it does is show a lot about your insecurity. The root cause of the problem facing many women with this mind frame is that because they have waited so long to become financial sable and put their career first without any focus on a relationship, they become financially able and lonely. Many women are, apparently, insecure when it comes to how much money they make. Obviously, like everybody else, women believe that making more money makes them a better person. Money doesn't make a person better; it just gives them more to spend to cover their insecurity. The concern about their jobs even plays a role in their insecurity of meeting the expectations in the company and their male competition.

Women with good careers are very insecure, which sometimes make them competitive to their male counter-partner. A man, yes, he does look at the type of job a woman has, but if they want you, it should not matter. Women here are some red flags to watch out for:

A *Woman's* Insecurities

If you meet a man and the first question out of his mouth, what type of work you do?; If money is the focal point of your conversation; if he brags on how much he paid for his car and/or clothing; and lastly, if he look to you to pay the bill, I don't care if its Burger King you run and I mean fast. Rather than worried about if you have enough money just to look good or even try to please a man, you should be secured enough within yourself and know that if that's his goal to use you for money, you can always do better, he's not the only man GOD made. Just think! Maybe "he is not your cup of tea."

What to do? Women keep your money conversation to yourself. Everything is not always for sale. Try trusting in yourself, without thinking about money makes you a better person. Don't put pressure where it doesn't have to be. Most importantly, focus on the positive and stop being fearful of becoming involved, and don't let money control your life, control it!

Not intellectual enough.

An intellectual life involves a person's ability to think and understand complicated ideas. Certainly, women are insecure about their level of understanding regarding various matters such as their reception and the pleasing of men. Distinctive qualities in an intellectual woman unfolds her mental skills, which she demonstrates; focus on the abstract, philosophical and esoteric aspects of her human inquiry and the value of her thinking. Women tend to be very critical in the way they grasp the notion of things, especially in their relationship. Having an intellectual life causes women to question their insecurity about their self-worth, appearances and what a real woman really should be concerned about. Women want men to think they have crossed all their "t" s' and dotted all their "I" s' to show themselves as a woman who have it all together. But the true is, as women, we are like everyone else, we have insecure issues within our social skills.

Psychologically, women tend to have a fear of embarrassment and failure, thinking that their intellectual content could impede their decision-making skills as well as affect their quality of choices. In a relationship, women develop a certain type of rejection behavioral trait that makes her feel guilty of having a man at the same intellectual level and understanding how to please him, which ends up ruining her relationship.

What to do: First of all, you need to know being an intellectual woman does not make you better than the next woman. Intellectual women have a distinctive quality about themselves that is mentally tamed through their demonstration of being positively philosophical in their esoteric aspects of human inquiries and valued thinking. So, standing up for yourself shows what a woman is really concerned about and can diminish what a man or anyone else may think about you. As long as you are secured within yourself and know what you know and even if you want to go and research for yourself, don't let others define who you are, let them see what you stand for. ("A Real Woman")

Healthy relationships are made up of secure people who create emotional energy to give to their partner, not take away from their emotional energy. Women who possess a quality relationship have been known to produce a better indicator of good health, just as a matter of emotional energy gives women positive nourishment in her soul, giving her confidence and security. When a woman has made successful transitions within her provisions of adulthood by learning to take care of herself, her maturation of emotional energy for self is well learned.

"A woman who learns to create her own energy is far free to give her excess to other women."

Dr. Arletha 'Angel' Lands

Overcoming Insecurity in Her Relationship:

Being insecure is part of the human experience. It's also the root of problems in a relationship. Insecurity in relationships is a fear-based emotion that causes mistrust. Insecurity not only hampers the relationship but crashes its validity. Overcoming insecurity in a relationship takes dedication and honesty from both parties. One of the most important things we need to understand in overcoming insecurity within a relationship is communication and trust.

Communication is a very integral part of making your partner feel secure as well as give them positive solutions. Insecurity in relationships also encompasses a sort of derivative type fear and jealousy that creates disaster. You see some of the reasons how jealous can lead into an insecure relationship is by having a poor self-image or low self-confidence, not thinking you are good enough or deserve the best; experiences in past infidelity, becoming use to unfaithful partners and thinking everyone is the same; and thinking the 'grass is green on the other side,' by looking at something that you think is better for you and dismiss the person you're with, and for someone you're not sure of.

Entering a relationship and having an insecure mindset provokes negative scenarios of rejection and immediate termination. However, in order to have a healthy and vibrant relationship, a person will need to develop trust. Without trust, there is really no relationship. Trusting each other carries the mount and shell of the relationship. However, a woman must realize that trust is not instantly developed, it is built overtime. For instance, allowing each other the willingness to reveal who they are, and show their integrity, if they have it.

There are several ways you can know that **trust** has been established.

- Having emotional security by letting your partner freely relax in the relationship without faulting.

- Let the intimacy between you and your partner grow and enjoy one another.

Overcoming insecurity in relationships as mentioned earlier is a difficult task for women and takes the deep development of a positive mindset. But do know that insecurity can be overcome if women are willing to try. As women, we must decide if we want a great relationship. If our intentions are positive, use these ideas below and act to benefit you and your partner.

1. Focus on the positive things in your relationship and build on it. Now, if your insecurities are due to real facts like caught cheating, mental abuse, and physical abuse, then re-evaluate the relationship and leave immediately. On the other hand, if you are just a woman who carries a pattern of insecurities in your relationships, then try to recognize where your problem comes from. It could be a matter of missing self-love.

2. Develop a positive mindset by learning how to positively view your relationship and stop thinking it's to be perfect. Stop creating and focusing on a wrong something that's not there and stops sabotaging the relationship and choose to imagine and think the best.

3. Stop the comparison game in present and past relationships. Many times, we as women think we're building bonus points with the new guy with talking about our past relationship, but all we are doing is

making him realize and thank GOD you was not in a relationship with him. So let your relationship stands on it's on and leave Harold, Henry, and Hector in the past.

4. Accept yourself for who you are by loving you and thinking good thoughts. The more you immerse yourself with love, it spreads around you and to the people you care about.

5. Develop positive self-assurance within yourself by living a happy life and then sharing it.

Women that become a couple always take the chance of becoming reactivated in their behavior of the partner, especially if self-esteem is lacking. However, women must still understand that the relationship can pull out their insecure side if not careful. Many times, women love the fact that guys show their vulnerability from time-to-time, but not for a long time. But also, she must know that her insecurities in the relationship stem from her own personal issues. See it's not that she turned insecure when she got in the relationship, that just some of her own baggage she carries and doesn't want to empty it.

Overcoming insecurities in your relationship takes understanding of why, what, and how you became insecure. Sometimes it is a mere measure of how we see ourselves as women. For example, we first start off by asking ourselves questions like, do he really like? Is he really interested in me for me? Will he cheat on me? Now remember you can come up with these questions on your own, he was not there physically with you to even ask such mess. Moreover, this is the kind of stuff that puts you in the negative mindset. With this type of attitude, it shows that you are extremely needy and desperate for a man's affection and can't bear the thought of losing his love. Now this is sad becomes you then becomes a dependent on him and his thoughts in order to be complete. But how can we fix it? By adopting a new mindset! You see a man want a woman who can demonstrate confidence and is secure within herself. So, if you really want your relationship, then get rid of the negative behavior that create problems and then stop trying to buy him; stop being possessive and jealous; and most importantly, stop demanding him to give you time and attention, because if he really loves you or have great interest, he will make the time as well as give you all the attention you need.

Insecurity in relationships is an ugly beast. It causes women to have feelings of inadequacy and low self-image, which is destructive to a woman's mindset. Insecurity also creates an overactive imagination. For example, women tend to overly imagine that their man is interested in other women, when he is not, letting their imagination get the best of them. That is why women should focus on what is reality and look at what's in the front of them and not imagining anything negative, especially regarding other women. Women should have some esteem about their self. Another problem with why we as women cannot overcome the insecurity in our relationships is because we don't allow our relationship to naturally progress. For instance, rather than waiting on the relationship to move to the next level in a normal and healthy way, we tend to force the relationship out of fear of losing that man who we desperately desire and love. But understand women, when forcing any relationship to move unnaturally because of your fear not only destroys it and make the other partner leave, because it is not beneficial for you or the person you are dating. All of a sudden, someone in the relationship became scared and bounced out of the relationship.

Overcoming insecurity in a relationship also takes a non-snooping personality. For instance, when he leaves his phone or wallet on the dress or table, you look in it for another women

A *Woman's* Insecurities

information. Many times, insecure women tend to snoop around, putting themselves in a 'sneaky person' category.

However, by doing so, these types of women mostly end up receiving the wrong message and set their self-up for confusion and distress for nothing. Why not live a stress-free life? Don't you deserve it? Look if a man wants you, stop worrying and let him put in his energy. Why don't you just give that man a chance to show you that he's interested? As I mentioned earlier, focus on positive experiences you have with him and see where that takes you. If it takes you to the next level, then go for it. If not, he is not the only man on earth GOD made. There is someone made especially for you, who knows how to handle your good and bad. Instantly becoming a mind reader or at least think you are, is a type of insecurity women that you should avoid bringing to the relationship. See, we as women fear the worse in our relationships by living in constant fear of trying to figure out if the man is interested in us. This type of mindset is definitely a driver of insanity. If you are that insecure about his interest, why not woman up and ask him, and be able to receive whatever answer he gives, then move forward. It's just that simple, ladies! Look, not every man you desire is interested in you, learn to move on to the next and stop crucifying yourself, causing unwanted heartaches and confusion.

Again, remember women we should avoid comparing our past relationships to the present. Listen, the guy that hurt you by cheating on you in the past is not the guy you are dating in the present. However, it is understandable that you feel a sort of insecurity because your feelings were hurt, and trust was broken with that person. But for the most part, get a grip and appreciated the relationship you have in the present and stop thinking every man is out to hurt you. Just remember women, being insecure in a relationship will only damage it. Think about this: We fall in love sometimes for the wrong reasons, by forcing a relationship progression; we become frustrated and confused in our choices, hoping intimacy will cover our flaws; and we become optimist in our relationship, by thinking negatively, all to do what but fail in our journey of finding the right love. *"CHANGE YOUR BEHAVIOR." When it's all done, it's only you that can set the stage for a positive invitation.*

Key Points for Overcoming Insecurity in Relationships

Women we know that overcoming insecurity in relationships can be a shaky situation because it creates a self-perpetuating series of events that is constantly repeated. Insecurity causes partners to become clingy and over barren, which worsen over time. In most cases insecurity in relationships often begins with family issues, and unhealthy relationships which interfere with a woman's ability to engage within a positive relationship. Although in some cases therapy is needed, there are several steps that women can take to reduce it until otherwise gotten over it.

Stop trying to Read his mind:

Many women tend to think that they are mind readers because GOD has given us the gift of discernment, but this is not what we should do. Remember too people don't exactly think alike even though they may think of a similar idea. In most cases, ladies' things that are said by man may come off in the wrong way which causes us to make our own assumption to what it means. But in reality, what we should do if we did not understand something or if something is bothering us, we should express our concern and ask for clarification and not ratification.

Learn to negotiate the rules in a relationship:

Women rules are set for standard purposes in a relationship, especially if you want it to work. You see each partner has their own prerogative in how they do things in a relationship and that's what makes them opposite but attractive to one another. But this is also to say that their own prerogatives should meet the needs of each other. For instance, agreeing on the same things may not be the same but the alternatives should meet in between the two so that each partner will feel if though they both are on the same team. However, when one partner feels some type of insecurity you or the other partner should be able to reassure that person by being able to talk openly and honestly about what is going on in order to make the relationship work. But if there is a disagreement regarding the constitutional and fundamental needs of each other, maybe this relationship may not be for you, 'Bounce' girlfriend.

Don't compare your relationship:

Look women! We see many good, bad, and ugly relationships everywhere. But for some reason we tend to want our relationship to be like that beautiful soap opera we see on T.V. in 'days of our lives.'

Okay let's wake up now! Women we need to stop comparing our relationships to what we may see or think on the outside as a "perfect" relationship as well as avoid comparing our current and past relationships. You see we tend to look for our partners' weaknesses and come to an assumption that they don't love us for who we are, but more likely you are comparing them to your past experiences which is not fair to them. Now if your partner tells you he/she loves you for whom you are, why can't you accept that and continue on with the positives and leave the negatives. You know many times when we try and emulate a relationship that may not even be real, we tend to make our relationship miserable and in up breaking up. So, work with what you have until it shows you different because if "it's not broke stop trying to fix it."

Look for the positive in your relationship:

A Woman's Insecurities

Women I have to say we look for anything negative first before we find the positive attributes in our partners. Look I know we are emotional creatures, but we are also psychologically determined to find evidence on rather or not our partners love us, cheating on us or just plain insecure within ourselves and don't know how to shake it from the past. See what we should do is focus on the positive attributes in our partners until he shows you otherwise as well as look at things positively so we can move past our own insecurities. Now I'm not saying let your partner use you or you ignore what he is doing, but just keep your focus positive and stay invigorating on a daily basis and you will see how it feds your partner by letting him know that he have a good woman that knows she is good and confident in her own self-worth. "Girl you got this."

A Fear of Relationship Commitment:

Fear has always been an issue amongst the many things we see that can hurt us, physically or emotionally. But when it comes to any type of relationship, fear sets at the forefront of our minds. You see as women, especially experienced women, having a committed relationship is like a life decision we make. As women we see commitment as a stigma that we have to keep because our word is our bond. Well, that's true but in this case many women see the practice of having strings attached is scary. A lot of women in their lifetime has seen as well as experienced the one-night stands and okaying thoughts of no-strings attached type relationships where there are no emotions but frivolous sex. However, we are clueless of the detrimental effects we portray in society as well as sabotage ourselves to remain commitment free. In other words, with being commitment free you convince yourself that it's okay. Until you realize that you have become soulless and disassociated from humanity. Well, if that's the choice you make don't complain or get jealous of the next woman relationship. Women, I know commitment is a scary word and it test our feelings of emotions, but is that's the real reason you want commit? But I think some of the reasons why women don't commit is because of their vulnerability, unrealistic expectations, time it takes, feeling of being trapped, pursuit of something better, negative experiences in the past, and schedule is too busy.

Let's speak to a woman's vulnerability. You see as women we are very emotional creatures and when we commit it is a 100% devotion of our being. But this is the scary part because when women do this type of commitment her pride is opened up and laid out for what may come next, whether it's hurt, good or bad. Now with that understanding, women we know in everything we commit to, rather buying a car, house, getting a new job or starting a new relationship we take the risk of being hurt. But this does not mean we should shut down. We must remember that all experiences, negative or positive are learning experiences that help us to grow by letting ourselves be vulnerable from time to time.

Sometimes we have to step out and take the risks; of course, with careful watch, but give things a try, because what we may think is the same negative experiences from the past, may be something that improves our character and knowledge in life. Just do you and if it doesn't work, keep doing it for you until it does.

Listen ladies, there will always be unrealistic expectations from time to time but don't let that take you by surprise! You see we are also creatures of habit where we sometimes crave mostly for what we can't have and turn down what we can have. I will tell you this, there is no perfect relationship, unless you are dating "GOD", and you know that answer. However, I think sometimes we women forget our reality and need to check ourselves. Stop trying to find Mr. Perfect, you know the one that you think fits all of your criteria, just don't put your eggs all in one basket, peel them one at a time, because I can tell you now that the chances of a Mr. Perfect doesn't exist.

Time is of the essences is said to be true because GOD holds time not human. In everything we do time is at the top of how it's done and when it's done. Look ladies, when we want something, we go for it regardless of the time it takes to get it, right? Now the same energy we put into what we want is the same energy we should put into our relationship. You see time once gone can never be gotten back, so why waste it. If a relationship does not work for you, stop there and keep it moving because time doesn't wait on you, and you don't wait on it. In another aspect of your life, having a busy schedule is always used in the front of commitment. It's not that you are too busy; you just don't want to take out the time to genuinely connect with someone. You just keep telling yourself, if I have time I'll do it, but you know that's a lie. There is no such thing as being too busy to enjoy different aspects of your life if you organize your time. Just speak the truth, you're just an introvert. Because all you need to do is manage your time, cut out the negative things surrounding you and organize your time efficiently.

You know it is very irritating when a woman feels trapped in a relationship that turned bad. Many times, she just stays in it and complains about it, letting others know how she feels stuck and how she is suffocating in her relationship, but she still is going back to it on a daily basis. Oh well, must not be TOO bad she's still in it. So, ladies if you are not going to make any changes and are stuck on "stupid" stop telling everybody your business because it makes you look stupid. Look either you stick it out, make changes or something because you are never trapped as much as you think you are, it is you that need to make that move. What I do know from experience is that we are always in pursuit of something better. But we have to remember not to be so competitive, always in competition. If you are pursuing a new relationship don't treat it like playing cards as soon as that card gets low, you want the higher card. Look commitment is not a game and so is a person's life. You never know the person you may give up because you think they are bad for your reputation and the person you chose thinking they are an upgrade, may be the worst mistake in your life. So, stop thinking you need to drop one thing in exchange for the other, everything that looks gold is sometimes plated.

Fear of Relationship Commitment Test

Fear of commitment is a major cause of breakups in romantic relationships. You have one person ready to tie the knot and the other person is not. Let's see if you are ready to take the plunge of commitment by taking this commitment readiness test. The test is made up of two types of questions: scenarios and self-assessment. For each scenario answer according to how you would most likely behave in a similar situation. For the self-assessment questions, indicate the degree to which the given statements apply to you. In order to receive the most accurate results, please answer each question as honestly as possible. Take the 20 minutes, it's worth it women.

(please check the appropriate box for each question)	Completely true	Mostly true	Somewhat true/false	Mostly false	Completely false
I am willing to do everything I can to support my partner.					
I accept the fact that in a committed relationship, I may occasionally have to sacrifice my own needs/dreams					
The success of my relationship takes priority over any other aspect of my life.					
If things were to end between my partner and me, it wouldn't bother me at all.					
Making sure my partner is happy is extremely important to me.					
I think my partner is the one.					
Whenever I make plans for the future, I take my partner into consideration as well.					

I feel that being in a relationship will interfere with the goals I want to accomplish.					
I look forward to seeing what the future holds for my partner and I.					
It's hard for me to picture my life without a partner.					
Being in a committed relationship involves a lot of responsibility that I don't want on my shoulders.					
I'm afraid that once I make a commitment to a partner, I'll lose my freedom or identity.					
It would bother me if my partner became dependent upon me (financially, emotionally, etc.).					
Once I'm in a committed relationship, I believe I will lose my privacy.					
I refuse to put my partner's needs before those of my friends or family.					
I refuse to put my partner's needs before my own.					
I think that being in a committed relationship is just too much work.					
Committing to one person will prevent me from meeting someone better.					
When in a serious relationship, I fear that I'll get hurt.					
I'm afraid that I won't be able to live up to my partner's expectations.					
I would have difficulty relying on my partner (financially, emotionally, etc.)					
I have difficulty trusting people.					

A Woman's Insecurities

With the frequency of divorces rising, I'm afraid that my relationship will end badly.					
If I were to commit to my partner, I'd fear I'd be making a mistake.					
It would bother me if I got attached to people very easily.					
When my past relationships ended, I had a lot of difficulty letting go emotionally.					
I am fearful that my partner will leave me for someone better.					
I'm afraid that once I'm in a committed relationship, it won't end up being all that I imagined.					
I think I'm better off not committing because I'll probably mess up the relationship somehow.					

Situational Fear of Actions Part 2

Your partner is out of town visiting his/her grandparents one weekend. Saturday night you decide to go out and, lo and behold, you bump into an old flame (who is looking great). Needless to say, the old chemistry is there, and you are invited to spend the night at his/her place. What would you most likely do?

- Take up the offer, even though someone could possibly find out.
- Take up the offer without even worrying about the consequences.
- Take up the offer. My partner and I have already discussed and agreed upon a sexually open relationship.
- Decline with regret and spend the night fantasizing about what could have been.
- Politely decline – someone might see us.
- Politely decline; I wouldn't risk compromising my relationship with my partner.

You and your partner are getting ready for a fabulous night out with a group of friends when she/he quite suddenly starts to feel ill. It appears to be the onset of the flu, so she/he crawls into bed and refuses to budge. His/her symptoms seem to be pretty bad but won't require medical attention. You have really been looking forward to this night out. What would you do?

- Stay home to keep an eye on him/her.
- Stay home but feel somewhat resentful.
- Go out only if she/he insists.
- Go out regardless of whether she/he insists that I stay home.
- Tuck him/her in and then go out.

A *Woman's* Insecurities

Stressful life changes and loads of work have put your relationship on the back burner. In fact, you haven't had sex in a month. It seems that things have become distant between you and your partner. What would be your most likely approach?

- o   Arrange to see a couple's counselor.
- o   Discuss the situation with your partner and try to figure out ways to rekindle the relationship.
- o   Sacrifice some of your responsibilities so you can make more time for your partner.
- o   Wait until your partner brings up the issue or does something about it.
- o   Nothing – whatever happens! happens!
- o   Break it off – you simply don't have time for each other.

Which of the following statements best describes your life?

- o   I don't even have enough energy to keep my own life together, let alone care for someone else.
- o   I have barely enough energy to keep my own life together – very little is left for somebody else.
- o   I'm in no hurry to open up my life to someone else, but if the opportunity comes along, I won't turn it down.
- o   I may be preoccupied with my own life sometimes but I'm generally ready to open up my life to someone else.
- o   I am totally ready to open my life to someone else.

If you were to stay with your partner for the long haul, she/he would have to:

- o   Change a few minor things about him/her.
- o   Change some things about him/her.

- Change several things about him/her.
- Change almost everything about him/her.
- She/he wouldn't have to change a thing about him/her.

You have a rather unfulfilling career but are otherwise basically quite settled where you live. Your partner just got an excellent job offer in another part of the country and would love to seize the opportunity. She/he asks you to join him/her and offers financial support until you've found another job. Leaving would mean saying goodbye to friends and family. What would you do?

- Go with my partner readily.
- Go with my partner, but with some reservations.
- Go with my partner knowing that I can always move back if it doesn't work out
- Go with my partner somewhat bitterly.
- Stay behind, planning to join him/her soon.
- Stay behind and try to work out a long-distance relationship.
- Stay behind and end the relationship

When thinking ahead 5 years, how does your partner factor into your life?

- She/he is part of all my future plans
- She/he is part of most of my future plans
- She/he is part of some of my future plans but for the most part, I'll be focusing on my own life.
- She/he has no part in any of my future plans.

While hunting for your own place, you discover a great apartment that is about 30% over your budget. Your

partner suggests renting it together. This not only means that you'll be able to afford it, but it also indicates that she/he intends to move in with you. What would you do?

- o I'd change my mind and rent something less fancy for myself.
- o I'd turn down his/her offer and lease it for myself. I'll just have to save as much as I can for rent.
- o I'd thank him/her for the offer and find a roommate instead.
- o I'd go for it. If things didn't work out id find another roommate or dip into my savings.
- o I'd go for it – I've actually been toying with the idea of moving in together for a while.

The thought of spending the rest of your life with your partner makes you feel:

- o Extremely uneasy
- o Fairly uneasy
- o Somewhat uneasy
- o Slightly uneasy
- o Not at all uneasy

How can women learn to love themselves?

Learning to love yourself is easily said than done. Many times, we as women admire other women and wish to be shaped liked her, be popular like her, walk like her, and even talk like her, if that's what we see as her success. ENOUGH! At this point, you are not even acting like a lady, less known a strong woman. You are not only not accepting yourself, but you are also degrading who you are, could be, and want to be. Your behavior is definitely characterized as low-self-esteem and no confidence in yourself as a person. How did you get to that point? Well for one, you must have been through so much in your lifetime that you cannot view the world as a positive setting that can offer you more.

Look, the world is yours, if you want it! The mistakes that women make in not loving themselves supplies and proves these facts: she is a negative and depressive woman, or must I say stupid person; she uses others to prove her status and still end up miserable, cause misery loves company; and she is definitely a sad case that no man want to be bother with or do for, all she can do is pay her way up, especially her so called man.

You see many times women who don't love and value themselves do things differently. They do things that affect them the most. Some things women do without value includes self-bashing; consistently doubting self; hang with the wrong crowd or social group; sabotage any success they may incur; become depended on others to make them happy; compare themselves to other women; and can't accept compliments.

A Woman's Insecurities

Self-bashing

With self-bashing women tend to place unrealistic expectations on their selves, especially when seeing other women who have it together. Look none of us women are perfect but whatever you esteem the most is what you ride on. But a woman with low grading values and a low self-esteem constantly picks at herself and is very hypercritical, making herself not to see any positive as well as proves she's not good enough for anything.

Consistently doubting self

Look we all have times when we doubt things and thinks we are not good enough, but women with no self-worth cripples her with a great self-doubt that she's too weak to stand up for herself because she thinks things want work out her way or even have what it takes to make it work. So, she just hides and feels worthless in her feelings about things and lets others walk on her.

Hang with the wrong crowd or social group

In many cases women who hang with the wrong crowd or social group is looking for acceptance and attention. Women who search for such acceptance see's popular people as a role model group to belong too. You see these women would do anything to be a part of something even if it means looking over any manipulation or abusive behavior from the group.

Sabotage any success they may incur

Women who sabotage their success believe they are not deserving of nothing good. Many times, they are afraid to achieve it because they my mess it up. They will convince themselves that they are a screw-up which makes them feel the facts of disappointing others and not just themselves.

Become dependent on others to make them happy

But the question you face, how can I learn to love myself? You may think learning to love yourself all of a sudden sprang on you, but it's not even the tip of the iceberg. Learning to love yourself stems from childhood teachings and positive reinforcements utilized in your family surroundings as well as the type of actions taken in the mist of your functional path. If you can think of a time, as a little girl, what negative or positive remodels participated in your life set the stage for your path. If the path was positive, you advance to a woman with self-dignity and self-confidence and if the path was negative, you progress by trying to fight your way through life, regardless to who you had to step on or use. See life does not always deal us a positive hand, as we grow older it is up to us women to learn how to change our negative behaviors to positive ones. I remember this saying by Mya Angelo, "when you know better, you do better." So, in that sense, by now you have realized that life is what you make it. BOOTH-UP GIRL...

INSECURITY IN RELATIONSHIPS SITUATIONAL CASES:

Talk About Abuse:

"Abuse"—is not the answer to a successful relationship OR POSITIVE self-dignity

In many cases, women who are insecure stay in abusive relationships. Why is this many ask? Well, unfortunately, woman who is insecure attracts men who are insecure, which means that abuse from men is taken easily by the woman who thinks nothing of herself and look to that type of attention. Looking at the situations below, who are you? Are you a Barbara, Brenda, Kathy, or Irene?

Situation 1:

Barbara has had a string of abusive boyfriends, but every time she gets rid of that one, she ends up with another one, just a different name, but the same. This means that she has so little confidence that she convinces herself that it's her fault and that's what she deserves. THIS IS WHAT WE CALLED THE *"SOLOWSHIP" woman.* So-low-ship is a woman who sees her self-worth as a mere entity for being abused by man as a way of showing their love for her.

Situation 2:

Brenda is a very beautiful woman that is self-starting in all business matters, a supervisor and leader of many groups and organizations and has her own home and owns her own car but has been in a relationship with a man for 20 plus years and never got married to him. The man she is with does not want to marry her but wants to continue getting the benefits and she continues giving it to him. Why is this? THIS IS WHAT WE CALLED THE *"NONENHANCED"* woman. This non-enhanced type of woman, believe or not, has a very low self-esteem but thinks she is in control of her situation.

Unfortunately, she has taken on the "bottom of the barrel" of disrespect for herself, low self-dignity and surely degrading her moral values.

A *Woman's* Insecurities

Situation 3:

Kathy is a very beautiful knock down gorgeous woman who have everything going for herself. She has a good job, loving family, home, expensive car, dresses nicely, but flaunts her sexuality as an attention getter to attractive men. THIS IS WHAT WE CALLED THE *"LOWCLASSIMAGE"* woman. A low-class-image woman like this is insecure in her efforts to seek constant validation from men which becomes her main source of emotional energy and how she defines herself. Rather than love herself inside, she searches for attention by putting material things to hide behind her low self-dignity.

Situation 4:

Irene is a classy woman who has been abused in every relationship, but don't care and has everything going for herself (job, home, car), but goes out and becomes sexually active with all the men she come in contact with. Irene not only seeks constant attention and shows a disparate need to have a man in her life, but her self-esteem is low and she has no emotional energy to reach higher goals. THIS IS WHAT WE CALLED THE *"PROJECTOR"* woman. This projector type of woman projects a needy desire to be loved at any cost which causes her insecurities to portray a lack of confidence in many dimensions of her daily life. She has no self-worth or dignity, even though she proclaims to have it ALL.

I hope you can see in these situations a woman insecurity in a relationship with a man can bring extreme sense of self-disrespect, low morale, low self-esteem, self-image, and self-worth. In other words, women seem to not understand the irrational jealous that men manifest and seek in their betrayal to just have sex. Men tend to manifest themselves in a constant questioning, mistrust and altercative pattern of respect for women.

You need to know, any man that abuses a woman have no respect or self-dignity as far as a woman is concern, and that goes for his mother and sister too. Because if he did he would be able to trust you, not depend on your well-being, or even is capable to forgive you. Moreover, if a man is abusive to a woman in a relationship also shows his insecurity that is extremely destructive out of his need for control.

WHO ARE YOU?

(PLEASE CHECK THE BOX BELOW TO IDENTIFY YOUR SITUATION IF APPLIES)

SOLOWSHIP	
NONENHANCED	
LOWCLASSIMAGE	
PROJECTOR	

HOW CAN I CHANGE MY SITUATION?

Building A Stronger & Secured Woman

Many times, we as women tend to let our loved ones, friends and societal influences implement the structure of our daily lives. Then we ask ourselves, why is this? But yet we discover a answer or even sometimes a method that equips us with the right tools and yet still implements negatives rather than enforcing the positives. Moreover, we tend to shut down our own GOD given insight as women and focus on negative past and present induced behaviors. But how can we overcome these mental mind breaking enthusiastic legions that holds a negative impact and erratic behaviors which keeps us from moving forward. Well, there are many things that we must recognized as women. First understand that GOD built you in a miraculous way which allows you to withstand something no man can do. For example, childbirth in which you have the capability to carry a whole human inside your body for 9 months if not a year and that's powerful. But also look at how the affirmation of your "CHAKRAS" which is a physiological practice built within your will to survive in spite of the odds. As women we have a GOD given intuition to visualize with a radiant, clear, and free flowing spirit for building a stronger and secured self. To build a stronger and secure you, you should focus on these affirmations in your life: Self-love; Confidence, Powerful Feminine, and Empowering affirmations.

Dr. Arletha Lands

REPEAT! REPEAT! REPEAT

THIS TO YOURSELF ON A DAILY BASIS

Today's Affirmations

CHAKRAS

I pledge to face all my insecurities and embrace the love and light of my self-being and self-image. I honor the willing energies I poses within my mind body and spirit as I continue reaching a secured self-development habit that brings me further into alignment with who I am made to be. I further will visualize my chakras radiant, positive, and clear understanding of how as a woman there shall not be insecurities against other women, men, or anyone or thing that embarks upon my energetic harmony for life.

Written by: Dr. A. Lands

A *Woman's* Insecurities

SELF-LOVE

Affirmation

I love...................
Myself
My life
My body
My hair
My skin
My eyes
My heart
My mind
My spirit
My soul
My laugh
My family
My friends
My silly sense of humor
I love to help others
I love to dance
I love to feel and inspire others around me

Written by: Dr. A. Lands

Dr. Arletha Lands

Affirmation For
CONFIDENCE

I am determined to reach my goals
I love who I am and who I am manifesting to be
I find strength in the midst of my vulnerabilities
I appreciate myself
I am standing beyond my past
I accept and love myself
I am powerful
I speak with confidence
I am enough
I am faithful to myself
I keep my body strong and full of energy
I am full of life
I arise with new energy and buoyancy
I am trustworthy
I attract positive friends
I attract people who help without a hidden agenda
I create positive relationships
I leave the past in the past
I look forward to better things in life

Written by: Dr. A. Lands

A *Woman's* Insecurities

Affirmation for
POWERFUL FEMININE

I am a very powerful and beautiful woman

I am capable of validating myself

I am bold and valuable

I am not a chaser, I'm an attractor

I believe within myself and knows what's best for me

I get rid of anything or anyone that brings me down

I exude top level confidence and positivity

I am a peaceful woman

I have a distinctive character that draws good people

I respect myself highly

I embrace positive energies around me

My happiness is priority

I take pride in showing my femininity

I expect the best in life, plus some

I have magnetic and irresistible energy

I know I am a queen

When I am done, I am done

Written by: Dr. A. Lands

AFFIRMATIONS FOR
EMPOWERING WOMEN

My problems are my teaching points of growth and realization in life

I have a strong will to finish

I am uniquely made

I refuse to give up

I deserve to be loved

I think with a grateful mindset

I hold no grudges, life is to short

I love giving

I have a forgiving spirit

I can overcome my obstacles

I have the power to change my own life

I am not perfect but strive to do better

Respect is a must for me

I am motivated

I embrace learning new things daily

I love life

I love to be loved

Written by: Dr. A. Lands

7-DAY
INSECURITY PROGRESSION TRACKING JOURNAL

THIS IS A DAILY PROGRESSION JOURNAL THAT HELPS WOMEN TO RECOGNIZE WHETHER THEY ARE INSECURED OR SECURED WITHIN THEIR SELF. IT ALSO PROVIDES YOU WITH ADEQUATE CONCERN ABOUT YOUR SELF-ESTEEM AND SELF-WORTH. SO BY KEEPING TRACK OF YOUR SELF- SECURITY IS IMPORTANT IN BUILDING YOUR SELF-CONFIDENCE AND CHANGING TO A POSITIVE BEHAVIOR.

Example:

Question	Pts	Yes	No	Comments
Did you talk about someone today?	4		x	
Did you think positive today?	5	x		
Did you think highly of yourself today?	5	x		
Did you say something encouraging to someone today?	4	x		
Did you feel depress today?	5		x	
Was your confidence level high today?	4	x		
Did you have any lack of trust within your self today?	5		x	
Did you have any fear of rejection or embarrassment today?	5		x	
Did you have any realistic expectation today?	5	x		
Did you focus on positive things today?	5	x		
Did you over use your authority today?	5		x	
Were you overly competitive today?	5		x	
Did you overly self-promote yourself today?	3	x		Stop showing off
Did you buy something you really can't afford just to be seen?	4		x	
Were you envious of anyone today?	5		x	
Did you have a good self-image of your appearance today?	5	x		
Did you show any jealousy of anyone today?	5		x	
Did you feel non-achievable against a successful person today?	2	x		Need to know I can do just as good/trust in myself
Did you feel unappreciated today?	2	x		I need to appreciate myself more
Did you have a positive mindset today?	5	x		
Were you self-assured today?	5	x		
I played the comparison game between my present and past relationship today?	4		x	
Did you become defensive today?	4		x	
Total Points	101			

Answer the questions above and write down your points for each question from the list below. Check yes or no to see where you are in building your self-esteem, self-confidence, and self-worth. Write in the comment section what you would like to change about yourself.

    5-Positive Self-Confidence   50-110 pts
    4-Building my self-esteem   49-34 pts
    3-Need more control over your attitude about being secured   48-30 pts
    2- I am poorly insecure in yourself   47-25 pts
    1-I have no self-confidence or self-worth, change my behavior   46-1 pts

On the back of this sheet, write something positive about yourself for today and date each entry.

Sunday:

Question	Pts	Yes	No	Comments
Did you talk about someone today?				
Did you think positive today?				
Did you think highly of yourself today?				
Did you say something encouraging to someone today?				
Did you feel depress today?				
Was your confidence level high today?				
Did you have any lack of trust within your self today?				
Did you have any fear of rejection or embarrassment today?				
Did you have any realistic expectation today?				
Did you focus on positive things today?				
Did you over use your authority today?				
Were you overly competitive today?				
Did you overly self-promote yourself today?				
Did you buy something you really can't afford just to be seen?				
Were you envious of anyone today?				
Did you have a good self-image of your appearance today?				
Did you show any jealousy of anyone today?				
Did you feel non-achievable against a successful person today?				
Did you feel unappreciated today?				
Did you have a positive mindset today?				
Were you self-assured today?				
I played the comparison game between my present and past relationship today?				
Did you become defensive today?				
Total Points				

Answer the questions above and write down your points for each question from the list below. Check yes or no to see where you are in building your self-esteem, self-confidence, and self-worth. Write in the comment section what you would like to change about yourself.

    5-Positive Self-Confidence   50-110 pts
    4-Building my self-esteem   49-34 pts
    3-Need more control over your attitude about being secured   48-30 pts
    2- I am poorly insecure in yourself   47-25 pts
    1-I have no self-confidence or self-worth, change my behavior   46-1 pts

On the back of this sheet, write something positive about yourself for today and date each entry.

Dr. Arletha Lands

Monday:

Question	Pts	Yes	No	Comments
Did you talk about someone today?				
Did you think positive today?				
Did you think highly of yourself today?				
Did you say something encouraging to someone today?				
Did you feel depress today?				
Was your confidence level high today?				
Did you have any lack of trust within your self today?				
Did you have any fear of rejection or embarrassment today?				
Did you have any realistic expectation today?				
Did you focus on positive things today?				
Did you over use your authority today?				
Were you overly competitive today?				
Did you overly self-promote yourself today?				
Did you buy something you really can't afford just to be seen?				
Were you envious of anyone today?				
Did you have a good self-image of your appearance today?				
Did you show any jealousy of anyone today?				
Did you feel non-achievable against a successful person today?				
Did you feel unappreciated today?				
Did you have a positive mindset today?				
Were you self-assured today?				
I played the comparison game between my present and past relationship today?				
Did you become defensive today?				
Total Points				

Answer the questions above and write down your points for each question from the list below. Check yes or no to see where you are in building your self-esteem, self-confidence, and self-worth. Write in the comment section what you would like to change about yourself.

5-Positive Self-Confidence   50-110 pts
4-Building my self-esteem   49-34 pts
3-Need more control over your attitude about being secured   48-30 pts
2- I am poorly insecure in yourself   47-25 pts
1-I have no self-confidence or self-worth, change my behavior   46-1 pts

On the back of this sheet, write something positive about yourself for today and date each entry.

Tuesday:

Question	Pts	Yes	No	Comments
Did you talk about someone today?				
Did you think positive today?				
Did you think highly of yourself today?				
Did you say something encouraging to someone today?				
Did you feel depress today?				
Was your confidence level high today?				
Did you have any lack of trust within your self today?				
Did you have any fear of rejection or embarrassment today?				
Did you have any realistic expectation today?				
Did you focus on positive things today?				
Did you over use your authority today?				
Were you overly competitive today?				
Did you overly self-promote yourself today?				
Did you buy something you really can't afford just to be seen?				
Were you envious of anyone today?				
Did you have a good self-image of your appearance today?				
Did you show any jealousy of anyone today?				
Did you feel non-achievable against a successful person today?				
Did you feel unappreciated today?				
Did you have a positive mindset today?				
Were you self-assured today?				
I played the comparison game between my present and past relationship today?				
Did you become defensive today?				
Total Points				

Answer the questions above and write down your points for each question from the list below. Check yes or no to see where you are in building your self-esteem, self-confidence, and self-worth. Write in the comment section what you would like to change about yourself.

    5-Positive Self-Confidence   50-110 pts
    4-Building my self-esteem   49-34 pts
    3-Need more control over your attitude about being secured   48-30 pts
    2- I am poorly insecure in yourself   47-25 pts
    1-I have no self-confidence or self-worth, change my behavior   46-1 pts

On the back of this sheet, write something positive about yourself for today and date each entry.

Wednesday:

Question	Pts	Yes	No	Comments
Did you talk about someone today?				
Did you think positive today?				
Did you think highly of yourself today?				
Did you say something encouraging to someone today?				
Did you feel depress today?				
Was your confidence level high today?				
Did you have any lack of trust within your self today?				
Did you have any fear of rejection or embarrassment today?				
Did you have any realistic expectation today?				
Did you focus on positive things today?				
Did you over use your authority today?				
Were you overly competitive today?				
Did you overly self-promote yourself today?				
Did you buy something you really can't afford just to be seen?				
Were you envious of anyone today?				
Did you have a good self-image of your appearance today?				
Did you show any jealousy of anyone today?				
Did you feel non-achievable against a successful person today?				
Did you feel unappreciated today?				
Did you have a positive mindset today?				
Were you self-assured today?				
I played the comparison game between my present and past relationship today?				
Did you become defensive today?				
Total Points				

Answer the questions above and write down your points for each question from the list below. Check yes or no to see where you are in building your self-esteem, self-confidence, and self-worth. Write in the comment section what you would like to change about yourself.

    5-Positive Self-Confidence   50-110 pts
    4-Building my self-esteem   49-34 pts
    3-Need more control over your attitude about being secured   48-30 pts
    2- I am poorly insecure in yourself   47-25 pts
    1-I have no self-confidence or self-worth, change my behavior   46-1 pts

On the back of this sheet, write something positive about yourself for today and date each entry.

Thursday:

Question	Pts	Yes	No	Comments
Did you talk about someone today?				
Did you think positive today?				
Did you think highly of yourself today?				
Did you say something encouraging to someone today?				
Did you feel depress today?				
Was your confidence level high today?				
Did you have any lack of trust within your self today?				
Did you have any fear of rejection or embarrassment today?				
Did you have any realistic expectation today?				
Did you focus on positive things today?				
Did you over use your authority today?				
Were you overly competitive today?				
Did you overly self-promote yourself today?				
Did you buy something you really can't afford just to be seen?				
Were you envious of anyone today?				
Did you have a good self-image of your appearance today?				
Did you show any jealousy of anyone today?				
Did you feel non-achievable against a successful person today?				
Did you feel unappreciated today?				
Did you have a positive mindset today?				
Were you self-assured today?				
I played the comparison game between my present and past relationship today?				
Did you become defensive today?				
Total Points				

Answer the questions above and write down your points for each question from the list below. Check yes or no to see where you are in building your self-esteem, self-confidence, and self-worth. Write in the comment section what you would like to change about yourself.

    5-Positive Self-Confidence   50-110 pts
    4-Building my self-esteem   49-34 pts
    3-Need more control over your attitude about being secured   48-30 pts
    2- I am poorly insecure in yourself   47-25 pts
    1-I have no self-confidence or self-worth, change my behavior   46-1 pts

On the back of this sheet, write something positive about yourself for today and date each entry.

Friday:

Question	Pts	Yes	No	Comments
Did you talk about someone today?				
Did you think positive today?				
Did you think highly of yourself today?				
Did you say something encouraging to someone today?				
Did you feel depress today?				
Was your confidence level high today?				
Did you have any lack of trust within your self today?				
Did you have any fear of rejection or embarrassment today?				
Did you have any realistic expectation today?				
Did you focus on positive things today?				
Did you over use your authority today?				
Were you overly competitive today?				
Did you overly self-promote yourself today?				
Did you buy something you really can't afford just to be seen?				
Were you envious of anyone today?				
Did you have a good self-image of your appearance today?				
Did you show any jealousy of anyone today?				
Did you feel non-achievable against a successful person today?				
Did you feel unappreciated today?				
Did you have a positive mindset today?				
Were you self-assured today?				
I played the comparison game between my present and past relationship today?				
Did you become defensive today?				
Total Points				

Answer the questions above and write down your points for each question from the list below. Check yes or no to see where you are in building your self-esteem, self-confidence, and self-worth. Write in the comment section what you would like to change about yourself.

    5-Positive Self-Confidence   50-110 pts
    4-Building my self-esteem   49-34 pts
    3-Need more control over your attitude about being secured   48-30 pts
    2- I am poorly insecure in yourself   47-25 pts
    1-I have no self-confidence or self-worth, change my behavior   46-1 pts

On the back of this sheet, write something positive about yourself for today and date each entry.

Saturday:

Question	Pts	Yes	No	Comments
Did you talk about someone today?				
Did you think positive today?				
Did you think highly of yourself today?				
Did you say something encouraging to someone today?				
Did you feel depress today?				
Was your confidence level high today?				
Did you have any lack of trust within your self today?				
Did you have any fear of rejection or embarrassment today?				
Did you have any realistic expectation today?				
Did you focus on positive things today?				
Did you over use your authority today?				
Were you overly competitive today?				
Did you overly self-promote yourself today?				
Did you buy something you really can't afford just to be seen?				
Were you envious of anyone today?				
Did you have a good self-image of your appearance today?				
Did you show any jealousy of anyone today?				
Did you feel non-achievable against a successful person today?				
Did you feel unappreciated today?				
Did you have a positive mindset today?				
Were you self-assured today?				
I played the comparison game between my present and past relationship today?				
Did you become defensive today?				
Total Points				

Answer the questions above and write down your points for each question from the list below. Check yes or no to see where you are in building your self-esteem, self-confidence, and self-worth. Write in the comment section what you would like to change about yourself.

    5-Positive Self-Confidence   50-110 pts
    4-Building my self-esteem   49-34 pts
    3-Need more control over your attitude about being secured   48-30 pts
    2- I am poorly insecure in yourself   47-25 pts
    1-I have no self-confidence or self-worth, change my behavior   46-1 pts

On the back of this sheet, write something positive about yourself for today and date each entry.

Dr. Arletha Lands

Certificate of Accomplishment

A Secured Woman

Upon recommendation of the book "A Woman's Insecurities" and the materials granted to esteem your knowledge of becoming a positive role model for insecure women as well as becoming a secured woman in your community, city, and state and among all women nationally

Acknowledges

_____

Name

With all rights, benefits and privileges appertaining thereto in recognition of your commitment to becoming a more secured woman about your self-image, self-worth and take the stand for your self-respect and women nationally

Accomplished on _____ *city* _____ *state, this* _____ *day of* _____ *month,* _____ *yr*

Secured Women Social Club Network (SWSCN)

Dr. Arletha Lands
Author of Book 'A Woman's Insecurities'